FRENCH TALES, TRAVELS AND TWO FOX TERRIERS

Mountains, Marmots and Much, Much More

Our French Odyssey
Book 2

JANE SMYTH

Foxy
Publications

Please note that this book is the original creation of the author. The author wrote and compiled it entirely without use of any artificial intelligence aid.

USE OF THIS BOOK FOR AI TRAINING:

Without in any way limiting the author's and publisher's exclusive rights under copyright, any use of this publication to "train" generative artificial intelligence (AI) technologies to generate text is expressly prohibited. The author reserves all rights to license uses of this work for generative AI training and development of machine learning language models.

**Foxy
Publications**

For the Love of Family …
"In family life, love is the oil that eases friction, the cement that binds closer
together, and the music that brings harmony."
- Friedrich Nietzsche

And the Love of Dogs.
"The truth I do not stretch or shove
When I state that the dog is full of love "
- Ogden Nash

Contents

Introduction

It's been a while. When I left you last time, we were all sharing life with that unwelcome newcomer, Covid-19 who, after we'd all been closeted in our homes for months, became a little evasive, hiding away and gearing up to launch yet another attack. It was during this lull that the final chapter of my book *French Dreams, Dogs and a Dodgy Motor* was concluded and everything was brought right up to date. However, life continues to happen, as does our story. As we bundle up our experiences and journey onwards, allow me to take you all along for the ride through a chronology of travels and tales, with a few asides for a sprinkle of reminiscences.

PART I

AUTUMN TALES

1

The Good and Bad of Things with Wings

I t was the middle of October 2020 and we were once again heading down to the house. Our gorgeous little property had now been embellished with a name, 'Les Hirondelles', for the swallows that regularly display their flying agility during the warmer months. While relaxing in the late afternoon sunshine, pre-dinner drink in hand, we watch as these cheerful little birds swoop back and forth with the skill of an aerobatic display team. Often they soar so high they become tiny specks in the sky before plunging back down at speed, continuing to amaze us as they whizz past our balcony. Their antics always make us smile, especially when they find themselves needing a moment's respite and choose one of the tall fir trees nearby in which to settle, or perch precariously on a telephone wire, chatting away to one another for all the world like a bunch of gossips on a street corner. On an invisible signal, they launch into the air once more to perform their airborne, insect-catching acrobatics, happily reducing the large population of annoying flies, many of whom seem determined to gain access to the house.

With fly screens on the windows and main door, we manage to keep many of these winged pests from entering, but those that get through will usually face annihilation. Sad I know, but I've tried to persuade the odd one or two to leave injury-free by offering escape through the open window or door, using a gentle scoop of the hand to guide them in the direction of fresh air. Of course, it's a complete failure as more fly in and those already in residence disappear deeper into the house ready to irritate the hell out of us by crawling up arms, legs or buzzing around our heads. Worse is their penchant for dining on a host of unsavoury things then kindly depositing regurgitated nasties on our food (I know this. I've seen that film *The Fly!*). Forgetting the humane approach, it was time to thwart the little sods once and for all. We attempted several methods. The Fly spray smelled awful and made the dogs sneeze, sticky tape wasn't sticky enough and the death lamp's 'irresistible attraction properties' proved 'resistible' as far as our flies were concerned as they happily ignored it.

In the end, I decided to purchase one of those tennis racket fly killers requiring a bit of practice and experimentation to achieve success. My initial attempts involved a lot of unnecessary energy. Spying one of the annoying, buzzing beasties lurking in the kitchen or sunbathing on the window glass, I'd run to grab the racket and slowly creep towards the offender. The annoying insect would spot me and take off before I got within range, so I'd resort to waving the racket through the air trying to swat it on the wing, often resulting in breakages and failure. I knew I needed to change my technique, discard the demented tennis player act and adopt a more subtle approach. I've since found that a gentle hover over the unsuspecting fly usually works. It being unaware of the threat from above, it will simply take off and conveniently commit suicide by heading into the electrified wire. For some odd reason, call it guilt, I always offer an apology to the corpse as I tip it into the bin. Rob, of course, thinks I'm beyond help.

Flies aside, Rob and I had tried to fathom a sensible name for the house for a while after others deemed 'The French House' a little lacklustre and boring. We agreed and once Rob was put in his place for suggesting 'Fawlty Towers', Les Hirondelles was born. In the end, it just seemed appropriate to name it after our little birds, even if there are quite a few properties called Les Hirondelles scattered around France. I know, because I searched on the internet.

2

The Paving Slab Story

Our ageing Landrover Discovery, which had recently celebrated its eleventh birthday, was still going strong but we had decided to leave it at home in the UK for our October trip. Roomy it might be, but on this occasion, it was impossible to squeeze in our luggage, two dogs and thirty Cotswold stone paving slabs I'd found advertised for free on a local neighbourhood website; a bargain too good to miss.

"I've found some lovely paving slabs" I gleefully told Rob, "and they're free!"

He looked nonplussed, obviously wondering why I'd developed the desire to lay a patio when we didn't need one. All was revealed when I suggested we take them to France to create a pathway across the pebbled area, which runs from the bottom of the steps to the door of the house. Any left could be used in front of the entrance to the sous-sol (cellar ... or as I call it, the 'spider hole'.) The slabs would help in keeping some of the weeds at bay which grow at an alarming rate, pushing up through the special liner we'd put down and the thick layer of stones placed on top. I seemed to be spending hours pulling the things out, apart from when everything was buried under a winter snowfall.

A week before we left for France, our Landy was put into service as we headed off to collect our new pathway. The dogs were left at home and seats were folded down to provide maximum space. The slabs had been stored outside, leaning against the side wall of a large, well-kept house situated in a very upmarket village not too far from where we lived in Worcestershire. The lady of the house explained the slabs had been surplus to requirements and had remained stored outside for months, getting in the way and looking unsightly.

She couldn't wait to be rid of them, so I immediately set forth, pulling one out from the pile, carrying it towards the car, very aware that said slab had a large amount of cobweb attached to the underside.

"Rob!!!!!" I shouted.

"What is it?"

"Cobwebs!" I bawled across at him.

"And? There's bound to be old web, dead leaves, dust and dirt as the slabs have been hanging around for months."

With my heart going nineteen to the dozen, I swiftly handed it to Rob before being tempted to throw the thing on the ground. I had a suspicion that a spider was lurking, ready to make a dash for it, most likely in my direction, especially as I was cuddling the slab against my chest to counter the weight. My heart started to thump at the prospect of encountering this creature as it ventured from its hiding place, wondering why its home was suddenly suffering a minor earthquake. In a bid for freedom, my face would be the designated escape route resulting in an outburst of noisy hysteria, a dropped slab, broken toes and a demonstration of some wild dance moves. I needed to proceed quickly before my imaginings became a reality.

Once this cobweb-infested piece of stone was safely stowed in the car, I spotted the eight-legged culprit making its escape. This would have been sufferable if the arachnid was heading out of the vehicle, but it was racing towards the front seats. Now those of you who read my previous book will know I hate spiders and dissolve in terror if one gets too close. I found myself trying very hard not to be an embarrassment in front of the nice family who had gathered to supervise proceedings. At first, I attempted to pass meaningful looks at Rob, trying hard to indicate he needed to do something. He regarded me with his own look which clearly demonstrated he had no idea why my face was distorting through a range of weird expressions aimed in his direction. With one eye on the spider, which was now teetering on the gap behind the seats soon to disappear into its depths, I edged closer to my husband and hissed in his ear to get the thing out of there … now!

"For Heaven's sake Jane, it's hardly a tarantula, it'll find its way out eventually."

"No it won't! It'll be living in the car and if it makes an appearance when I'm driving then I'll go into a complete meltdown and probably wind up killing myself or some other poor sod. I'm sorry, you've got to get it out."

I retired to a safe distance, but not too far as I needed to monitor progress. I could see my frustrated husband doing his best to persuade the spider to return to the outside world by gently nudging it with a small stick. He won't handle a spider saying he's not frightened of them, but wouldn't choose one as a pet, isn't keen on them and would prefer not to have one running up his arm. After a bit of zig-zagging, the obliging spider slowly meandered towards the open tailgate. A gentle flick and it was soon running happily towards the hedgerow. I breathed an enormous sigh of relief that it had 1) been ejected and 2) was still alive. I hate the thought of killing one. Doesn't seem fair as the rational side of my brain tells me the spider won't hurt me as we're not in Australia, but the irrational side of my brain tells me the spider will purposely seek me out, scurry over my face and try to crawl up my nose. I should never have gone to the cinema to see *Arachnophobia*! There is a positive side though … they eat flies!

From then on, with the help of a loaned broom, a hand brush and the family's strong son-in-law, the remainder of the slabs were loaded, brushed free of all cobwebs and securely stacked in the car.

3

First Night – Anybody There?

We made the decision to travel to France in Rob's large company van. It had a ton of room in the back and two rows of seats in the front, perfect for us, the dogs, the slabs and a load of other paraphernalia we presumed we'd need. I'd booked our first overnight stop in a small hotel not far from St Omer and had received the confirmation. Positioned on the corner of two roads in a fairly non-descript small town, the premises looked fairly unpresuming and very quiet. Stone steps lead to the front door directly off the street. Leaving the van in a public parking area opposite, we strolled across the road to enter but found it locked. We knocked and waited. Nothing. We peered through the windows to see if we could spot signs of life. Nothing. We walked around the corner and found an alternate entrance, but that was locked too. "Are you sure we're in the right place?" queried Rob. "It's a bit strange there's no one here."

We had arrived in the early evening. The town was small with no obvious sign of additional lodging, so we resorted to telephoning the number on the confirmation email. A jolly French lady answered who seemed completely at ease with the fact she'd been expecting us and hadn't turned up. It didn't bode well. *"J'arrive!"* she shouted down the phone. Ten minutes later the door opened. A young lady, not looking particularly pleased, with a voice that certainly didn't match the one we'd heard on the telephone, escorted us to our room and told us if we wanted to eat, we could dine in the restaurant which was due to open at 7.00 pm and left us to it.

"Well, that was strange," I said to Rob. "She was a bit grumpy. Think that lady we talked to on the phone was the boss and the receptionist was caught cat-napping?"

"Maybe", Rob responded "but we're here now and it doesn't look that bad. C'mon, grab your coat, the dogs are in need of a pee and a walk. We've only half an hour before the restaurant opens and I'm starving.

The autumn evening was gradually fading into night. In another hour it would be dark and cold, so we needed to get a move on. Looking through our first-floor window we could see what appeared to be a park, opposite. Leaving the hotel we headed across and entered through some ornate gates, affixed to which was a notice displaying the opening and closing times, reassuring us we'd not risk the danger of being locked in. After managing to get locked into the Tuilleries Gardens in Paris many moons ago, we always double-check such things.

In the middle of an expanse of grass and flower beds stood a large manor house which looked to be used as some kind of public building or offices. We meandered past its car park and headed for the woodland to the rear, hoping we would not be faced with an irate French person yelling at us for trespassing on private property. Following a small pathway which climbed steeply between the trees, we found ourselves surrounded by silence as we ventured further into the gloom, kicking up the damp autumn leaves as we went. The dogs were delighting in being out of the car, running around, exploring the undergrowth as we kept a close eye on them.

Teddy is a bit of a hunter and once he gets a whiff of fox or rabbit, he's off like a rocket. He's not keen on cats either! Maisie on the other hand, takes no notice whatsoever and wonders what all the fuss is about. She obviously thinks he's an idiot. Thankfully, it seemed that much of the wildlife was settling down for the evening before the nocturnal inhabitants rose from their slumbers and ventured forth. However, Teddy was on full alert and it wasn't long before he caught the scent of something needing urgent investigation. Like a shot, he plunged into the bushes, tramping about trying to locate whatever it was.

"You'd better go and get him." I said to Rob. "You know what he's like, he'll shoot off somewhere and it's getting dark. He'll also return in his own time, no doubt covered in something revolting."

"Why don't you get him?"

"Because it's your turn. The last time he ran off, it was me who spent an hour in the rain waiting for him to come back. I then spent another half an hour at home, attempting to clean him up."

Rob knew he'd lost the argument, so headed after Teddy, lead in hand. You could almost see Teddy's little brain plotting some fun as he eyed Rob creeping towards him.

"Wait!" Shouted Rob. "Teddy! Wait!"

I sensed what was about to happen as Teddy launched towards the top of the slope we'd climbed earlier. He paused long enough for Rob to almost grab him, but Teddy was enjoying this game of chase enormously and headed off down the slope, no doubt laughing to himself.

"Bloody hell Ted! Wait will you, you annoying dog!"

With Teddy now happily waiting at the bottom of the slope, tail wagging with enjoyment, Rob began to tentatively approach the slope which was slippery with wet leaves. Now Rob is a past master at slipping on a variety of surfaces: snow, mud, wet grass and sheep poo to name but a few. On this occasion, he added wet leaves to his list as he slid on down on his back to join Teddy at the bottom. By the time Maisie and I reached him he was back on his feet, covered in mud. Teddy had been secured on his lead without protest, Maisie was leaping about barking with joy at being reunited with Teddy and I was bent double with laughter. Rob wasn't happy.

"What are you laughing at! It's not funny. Have you seen the state of my jeans?" He uttered as he was trying to brush off the worst of it. "At least this hound of ours is on his lead at last, bloody animal."

He grumpily turned and walked back towards the gate, muttering to Teddy about how he would never, ever be allowed off his lead again. I followed on with Maisie, still giggling, not daring to mention the amount of mud clinging to the back of Rob's new jumper. He'd find out soon enough.

As the notice promised, we were able to leave the park without squeezing through the thick hedging surrounding it or scaling the pointy railings. The gate remained open and we made it back to the hotel in time for Rob to clean up, grab clean clothing and throw his mud covered garments into the back of the van. Teddy had polished his halo and behaved impeccably at dinner, lying quietly under the table with Maisie alongside. Rob forgave him and the "never, ever" punishment was revoked the next morning, allowing Teddy to run around the park with Maisie at his heels. He also earned a treat for being a good boy, at least for the time being!

4

Remembering a Tale from Long Ago

R ob and I have a marriage-long habit of innocently finding ourselves in ridiculous situations—a habit that hasn't diminished with age! When you've lived as long as I have, memories happily store themselves away in a very large filing cabinet in your head, waiting for the drawer to be unlocked, the file to be extracted and dusted off in readiness to be delved through once more.

Like a film reel, the images played out in my mind, revealing the events of a December evening long ago, when four of us found ourselves locked into the Tuilleries Gardens in Paris. Specifically why we decided to explore the gardens at such an hour has been lost in the mists of time, but what happened remains clear. I can still hear our voices from so long ago, probably consisting of more bad language than I've revealed here to avoid causing offence. I don't doubt for a minute that expletives were uttered many times as the adventure unfolded, but it was the laughter I remember the most—in my case, laughing so hard I almost wet myself. I know that laughing fits come highly recommended as they release all those delightful endorphins, helping to add a few extra years to your life, but they aren't a good idea if you have a full bladder and are in a location with nowhere to "go", like the top of a huge wall in Paris! Here's the story:

Rob and I were accompanied by Terry and Janice, Rob's brother and his wife. How we all managed to get ourselves into the situation was probably due to glugging too much wine at a late lunch, then swanning around the park, failing to check the time or notice how dark it was getting. We ambled towards the exit to find the gate locked. Mild panic ensued as the place was deathly quiet and totally deserted. We began a brief discussion about what to do, interrupted almost immediately when we spied two human figures emerging from the darkness. We locked onto them like a drowning person finding a life jacket. They, in turn, appeared to experience quite a shock at finding themselves accosted by four slightly desperate and over-jolly English tourists, asking in lamentable French for directions to get out of there. Looking a bit shifty and anxious to escape, they acknowledged the gates were *fermées,* before rushing off to disappear into the gloom once more. We wondered what the hell they were doing in the park after hours, but will leave you to draw your own conclusions.

With no other obvious choice, we decided to conduct an examination of the lofty perimeter wall and search for a suitable place to test our Spiderman skills by attempting to shimmy over it. After a walk alongside never-ending impenetrable stonework we stopped, eyed the wall and decided this was the spot. Our sanity and judgement had obviously done a runner. The wall towered above us. Rob was persuaded to go first. A lift from Tez and a certain amount of undignified scrabbling eventually found him sitting astride the top, disappearing slowly as he slid down the opposite side. A thud and a shout of "Made it!" indicated he'd succeeded without breaking any bones.

I went next, also with a bit of a shove-up from Tez, attempting to get a grip on the top of the wall and haul myself up. As I flailed around, legs swinging to gain more purchase, my one foot came to rest on the top of Tez's head, providing some stability and more height. I don't recommend using a head as a launchpad as it's quite difficult, especially if the head is wobbling and its owner is yelling "Gerrof!! That bloody hurts," while, at the same time trying to grab onto the leg the foot belongs to and push it off. Happily, the screams of pain subsided amidst grumbles about being scalped and I eventually hauled myself to the top. I peered at the drop on the opposite side, uttered several expletives and wondered if I'd make it down without wetting myself as my wine intake was now trying to make its exit. Rob looked up, "It'll be ok, hang on to the top of the wall and lower yourself down. I'll catch you." Nervous, but filled with alcoholic bravado, I slithered and giggled my way as far as my arms would stretch and trustingly let go. There was an "Ooofff" sound from Rob as I landed on him.

Then Janice started to panic. Rob and I could hear her saying there was no way she could do it. "I can't. I'm not good at that sort of thing and I'm in a skirt! I'll fall. I know I will. There's got to be another way out of here. C'mon Terry, please, can we go and look again?"

"No we bloody well can't," said a sore-headed Tez. "We've already been around the whole place and asked those two guys. For heaven's sake Jan, get a grip. No one is going to see your knickers except us. Do you really want to be stuck in here all night?"

Rob and I didn't help matters either by yelling a series of jokey comments and loudly singing *Humpty Dumpty* while tittering like a couple of school kids. It was good wine!

A solution was finally reached after a shouty discussion through the wall. Tez was to get himself to the top, with a small assist from Janice, and drag her up. The poor chap nearly burst a blood vessel with the effort as, suspended like a circus performer hanging onto a trapeze, Janice simply hadn't the strength in her arms to be of any help. With grunts and swearing from him, she finally reached the top, flopping onto it like a sack of potatoes. Resisting the demands of my bladder, I was helpless with laughter, which turned painful as the two brothers coaxed Janice down, Tez lowering her slowly while Rob was ready and waiting to support her knickered bottom, hoping she didn't fall on his head. She made it in one piece, vowing never to do something like that ever again, while I stood, legs crossed, urging a quick getaway to find relief. It remains one of those memories from our long-ago Paris trip that we still reminisce and laugh about today, as well as the Armenian and the mattress, but that's another story!

🐾

5

Arrival

After another long day on the road, we finally arrived at Les Hirondelles to find it still standing. There was no evidence that it had been used as a hunting ground by the odd mouse looking for an easy meal, nor of the insect population, except for a couple of dead flies in the sink. Usually, Mother Nature's unwanted house guests wait until we're there before making a nuisance of themselves.

Outside was another matter. Our small patch was covered in weeds, obviously delighting at the weather conditions during our absence to grow in strength, size and number. The few shrubs we possess seemed to have had a growth spurt similar to Jack's notorious beanstalk. As always it would be my job to deal with all this rampant greenery. Rob doesn't have a gardening bone in his body, though he will, occasionally, mow the lawn at home or give me a hand if I'm battling an enormous shrub which is fighting back. For now, our focus was to get settled in. Those slabs could wait until tomorrow to be unloaded.

The following morning, the weather remained kind. A wander onto the balcony to wake ourselves up with a lungful of fresh mountain air enabled us to take in the view. The valley was bathed in sunshine, the deep green pines lining the mountainsides were now interspersed with small pockets of blazing autumn colour, the final hurrah as the leaves breathe their last before winter sets in. I often think autumn is my favourite time of the year here, but it's hard to choose and I accept that every season in this beautiful place has something unique to offer that makes it so special.

We were snapped out of our reverie when Gilbert appeared and came over to chat.

"Bonjour mes amis. Avez-vous fait un bon voyage? Combien de temps restez-vous?"

We talked for a while, answering his questions about where we'd stayed or if we'd hit any traffic problems. We told him we were staying for two weeks, explaining we had some jobs to do. If anyone knows about working on these properties, it's Gilbert. He dons his work overalls and gets on with a seemingly endless list of tasks whenever he's in residence without Annie for company.

He recently removed his old bathroom, completely renovating it into a *salle de douche* (shower room). While undertaking this job, he'd often pop in to ask for permission to look into our shower room to gain some ideas and to see how this teeny-tiny room was configured. He was relieved when his own was finally finished, partly because it took forever, partly because he's not an expert plumber and partly because he was pleased with the result of his hard work. We were invited around to see it and admitted he'd done a great job.

Apart from internal house improvements, he cleans his own chimney and loves *maçonnerie* (stonework), hence his front door, which is a few feet lower than the track that passes by, has a neat set of steps and smooth walls alongside the drainage channel. His logs are dealt with efficiently, cut into sensible sizes for his log burner and stacked neatly outside to weather, before he brings them into a store room to dry out. When not concentrating on his slew of jobs, he'll be off on his bicycle, riding a circuitous route up mountain and down dale, or taking a hike with a walking friend from the village. His partner Annie admits she's not up to hiking these days, but they often go for a gentler walk together in the mountains along one of the marked trails. Gilbert admits, at his age (he's in his late seventies) he is beginning to slow down a little. He makes us feel like well-practised couch potatoes. At least he's given up the sport of running up and down mountains for fun. We think he's an absolute marvel and one of the nicest people we've ever met.

During our conversation, Gilbert pointed out something we'd completely missed. The cables that swung between a series of telegraph poles alongside our row of properties had gone, along with the ugly wooden pole planted dead opposite his balcony. We were delighted. They were an eyesore that we'd got used to over time, but now our field of vision was clear of horizontal lines. Gilbert was really pleased. That telegraph pole had been a real thorn in his side. My thoughts slid towards our swallows, who upon their return would be miffed to find their communal perch missing.

It seemed the burying of cables wasn't the only change. Along the small road that led the way through the commune, new lampposts had appeared. The ugly old ones had been disposed of, replaced with those befitting the foggy streets of London in Dickensian times. Thankfully, these were fitted with modern LED bulbs that didn't require the skills of a 'gas-lighter' gentleman. To see some form of modernity in our little backwater was encouraging. Maybe fast access cable would be next. We could only hope!

A New Neighbour

The following morning the slabs were removed from the van and left in a couple of piles near the door. Moving them proved to be a proper workout as we trundled back and forth, lugging the things up and down the steps. Job done, I then eyed the weeds. There was no getting out of it. They just had to come out. Rob conveniently disappeared inside kindly leaving me to it, offering to make lunch once he'd answered some work calls.

Work is Rob's stalker, one that avoids capture and imprisonment and pops up at the most inopportune times. He's often dealt with business calls on a ski lift, much to my irritation as he thrusts his ski poles at me to hang on to while he struggles to extract the mobile from the inside pocket of his ski jacket.

"Can't you switch that bloody phone off? Or just tell whoever it is you can't talk now because you're several feet in the air on a ski lift? Or better still, tell them you're on holiday and you'll deal with whatever it is when you get back!"

He totally ignores me of course, deals with whomever it is, whatever it is, and whenever it occurs.

I eventually finished pulling weeds and headed indoors with backache, broken nails and a sweaty face. The sun had snuck around the corner of the house and pushed the shadows to one side. My work area had been in full sun and even though it was October, it still left me slowly barbequing under its rays. I dreaded to think of the consequences without my factor fifty. Wrinkly, parchment-dry skin is not an attractive look. After scrubbing the dirt from under my remaining fingernails and washing my sweaty face, Rob served up a refreshingly crisp salad lunch, laced with a slice of Philippe's tasty herb-crusted ham, all washed down with a glass of rosé. We ate outside on the balcony, planning our slab laying tactics, unanimously agreeing to delay the job until the following day. For now, it was all about relaxation, the dogs showing approval by lying flat out in the shade, limbs twitching gently as Teddy dreamed about chasing balls and Maisie dreamed about chasing Teddy.

Slab Laying, Dog Naming

The slab laying began in earnest the next morning with Rob taking care they didn't look as if put there by an inebriated navvy. Later, the air turned temporarily blue as he discovered two slabs needed careful cutting to shape. It was the smallest of gaps, but angled and awkward. Typically, this was the last thing to be done. Gilbert had returned home to Cannes for a couple of days, so we would have to await his return and then hope he had a suitable tool for the job. With the air clearing as Rob began accepting this unforeseen hiccough, help arrived in the shape of our new neighbour who, after hearing from Rob about the problems he was having, announced he possessed a stone cutter and we could use it whenever we wanted.

We'd only met our new younger neighbour briefly, when he came to an aperitif at Gilbert and Annie's the previous summer, though we'd got to know his dog well as she appeared every day to pay her respects and play with our dogs. She was a young golden retriever who was given the name Gaia, the name for the Earth in Greek mythology. A nice, but strange name for a dog, but then we've met many a canine blessed with an odd or amusing moniker. These days it seems dogs have lost the traditional Fido to be replaced with names such as Hazel or Roger. Sci-Fi heroes also figure with Yoda and Loki being two we've encountered. Felines aren't immune either as I once knew a huge cat named Derek. We acted just in time to prevent Maisie from being called Muffin. Rob dug his heels in.

"No way! Can you imagine me having to call her back on a walk, especially if we shortened it to Muff. Even she'd be embarrassed!"

Our new neighbour, his wife and their two little girls had moved into a large chalet on the road above. It looked huge, with three floors, but the wooden façade had deteriorated over the years and now looked quite shabby and sad. We presumed it was bought as a bit of a doer-upper.

He was a great guy, speaking English like a native. We presumed he was in his early forties and discovered he and his family had moved from the Mediterranean coast to the mountains. He had that kind of super casual, floppy-haired rock star vibe about him, but this is me making assumptions as I doubt he spends his spare time blasting out guitar riffs while strutting around his living room. The only noise coming from his property is barking from an excited Gaia when someone passes by or his children's laughter as they play.

Rob immediately took up his offer of loaning the stone cutter and in a short amount of time our job was finally completed. With a few slabs left over, we used them to neaten up a tiny patch under the balcony, outside the sous-sol doorway. We were happy our commune had welcomed a new family into the fold, especially one that owned a huge array of tools we might be begging to borrow at some point in the future.

6

The Neighbours and the Tree

Gilbert was now the *Chef de Copropriété*. The wonderful Albert was forced to desert his long-held post and returned to his home on the coast where he passed away soon afterwards. Each time we arrive at Les Hirondelles and pass by Albert and Simone's little house, we feel their absence acutely. No more do we receive cheerful greetings and invitations to share an *apéritif* where we are privy to Albert's funny stories or Simone's updates on local gossip. We have such happy memories of times spent with this adorable older couple and will be forever grateful to them for the welcome and the friendship they extended towards us.

Gilbert takes his responsibility as seriously as Albert did and we are all summoned to the annual meeting of the *Copropriété* as required by law. Gilbert tries to arrange the meeting to coincide with one of our visits, but this isn't always possible and more often than not, others aren't in residence either so he often has to run it with maybe four present at most, sending out the agenda, voting form and accounts to non-attendees by email. There is never much we have to discuss or vote on, except for minor matters such as agreeing to someone building new steps or validating the accounts.

During the summer of 2018, Gilbert informed us one of the properties had been sold to a couple who resided in a small town further down the valley and were using the house exclusively as a holiday let. I caught sight of our new neighbours not long afterwards, wandered down to say hello, introduce ourselves as the local Brits and get the opportunity for a nose inside. I was simply curious to see how this property differed from our own, so was somewhat shocked to find it incredibly spartan. A woven chair, of the type you normally find suspended from a tree in the garden, was hanging from a beam in the centre of the room. A small rolled-up sofa bed, a tiny old-fashioned TV placed where no one could see it and a weeny log burner were the only contents of the living room. The kitchen area was old with dark brown cupboard doors and dark brown tiles giving the whole place a gloomy and unloved feel. I did wonder at the reaction of his clients upon entering such a bleak space. I'd have been mortified, but presumed they didn't mind. We were once told that the average French family don't require their holiday accommodation to resemble a glamourous *pied–a–terre*, preferring to adopt a more frugal attitude just as long as they have access to white goods. There is also much to do here in the mountains, keeping visitors busy exploring, playing or lazing in the great outdoors, greatly reducing any time spent lingering in the property. I also bet it was cheap to rent.

Keeping these thoughts to myself, a conversation took place in English which he spoke quite well. I remember explaining that all our properties were built to the same footprint, though differed inside according to the owners' wishes at the time. I'd received this reliable information from Albert, who had been present when construction was undertaken many years ago and who remained the keeper of all the original plans. Our newcomer disputed this quite forcefully, brooking no argument, his demeanour a tad condescending. I felt hackles rising and teeth gritting, so politely took my leave. Within our commune, we are surrounded by wonderful neighbours, but I firmly placed our newcomer into the category of 'wait and see'. Things didn't bode well when we found out during the summer of 2020 he had developed a bee in his bonnet about a tree which sat innocently on a neighbour's property.

The neighbour wasn't part of the co-op. The tree was reasonably small, and had the potential to increase in size, but proved to be no hazard or disrupter of views. At the annual meeting we'd managed to attend that year, our newcomer, in a show of self-importance, flourished several documents in the air before slapping them on the table, indicating he had investigated the legalities of demanding the tree's removal. It appeared he would need to spend quite a sum on a *notaire* (solicitor) to fight this, suggesting the best solution would be for the co-op members to share the costs, using their house insurance if necessary. Rob and I gave each other one of those 'raised eyebrow' looks, confirming we thought it was a right cheek of him to even think this.

Gilbert decided the best way to put this to bed was to get the opinion of all the residents. Meanwhile, Rob and I trotted over to see the arborous offender and stood beside the back of the newcomer's house to see what dreadful sin the tree had committed which required legal intervention and possible execution. The answer was nothing. It did not present any problem at all.

During the intervening time between summer and our return this October, everyone had voted against supporting the newcomer in his expensive and unnecessary quest. Why on earth would anyone, when the situation had no bearing upon them whatsoever, contribute towards legal costs accrued pursuing the death sentence for a totally innocent tree? He could pontificate all he liked!

Seeing Gilbert out and about one morning, we asked for an update. It involved bringing up an incident that had happened a couple of years earlier, when the possessor of the non-problematic tree had seen fit to extend his garden, taking a small slice of land belonging to the co-op. He proudly demonstrated his ownership by laying a neat pebbled surface for his table and chair, completing the job with a low fence, erected to show the division between what was 'his' and what was 'ours'. To be honest, no one was particularly bothered at the time, as the section was tiny, unused, unnoticeable and positioned down a small slope below a natural hedge. Taking land, however small, was illegal without signed permission and approval from residents.

Gilbert was dispatched to deal with it, explaining the land would need to be purchased for a small cost or handed back. He successfully extracted promises and dates for the land's return. Purchase was out of the question, our neighbour having concocted a multitude of excuses as to why. During the intervening period, nothing happened and the land remained in his possession.

In the end, we presumed poor Gilbert had been fed up with having to deal with the forceful demands from the newcomer and the boneheaded, foot-dragging attitude of the neighbour, so his resolution to the problem was to offer the neighbour a deal. If the tree was removed, he could keep his tiny bit of stolen territory. They shook hands on it and that was that, or so we thought. The foot-dragging continues to this day and all remains as it was, including the bottomless stock of excuses. The only change is the tree, happily receiving a stay of execution, continuing to grow steadily amidst the trouble and strife.

7

Off to Burgundy

Lockdown was the situation we all found ourselves in during the early part of 2020, with things easing during the summer. When we left the UK that October having had negative tests, acquired our proof of vaccination and completed a *Declaration d'Honneur,* serious faces were once again issuing dire warnings about another surge.

Two days before we left Les Hirondelles on our homeward run, we received a message from Bob, our friend who lives near Lyon, alerting us that France was enforcing a new wave of tougher restrictions once again, just in time for our journey home. We gave our overnight hotels a ring to confirm we wouldn't be forced to sleep in the car.

Our first night was spent in Fixin, (pronounced Fissan) a small village in the Côte d'Or. We'd stayed in the tiny ancient hotel several times in the past, primarily because the food was outstanding. Disappointingly, the restaurant was closed due to restrictions and we were the only guests in residence. Upon arrival, we engaged in a loud conversation with the owner at reception, trying to make ourselves heard, speech muffled by masks while standing at an exaggerated social distance. Informed we could still select our meal from the restaurant menu, we were issued with the old-fashioned key and told we would have to eat dinner in our room. When our meal finally arrived on the biggest tray I'd ever seen, I had to admire the dexterity of the chef who managed to manoeuvre it through the narrow doorway without having the contents slide off. He also avoided tripping over the dogs gathered at his feet, excited by the aromas of food wafting from under the shiny silver domes. He laid it carefully on a tiny corner table and left us to it after saying *"Bon Appetite"*. The dogs sat near as we ate, adopting their pitiful 'close to starvation' look in the hope we'd feel sorry and offer them something tasty from our plates. "No!" we said sternly.

It was, as expected, a fabulous meal. Concealed under two of the silver domes was a mouth-watering *Eggs en Muerette*, (eggs poached in a red wine sauce), one of my favourites and *Foie Gras* that Rob always chooses if it's on the menu. Starters were demolished in record time as we were so hungry after our long journey. Off came the remaining silver domes to reveal our main meal, a beautifully cooked *Pintard sauce Morilles*, (guinea fowl in wild morille mushroom cream sauce) with prettily arranged vegetables and potato gratin. It tasted divine. The guinea fowl was meltingly tender and the sauce beautifully rich with cream and the earthy taste of morille mushrooms. We almost licked the pattern from our plates. Maisie and Teddy hadn't moved a muscle, sitting patiently, their eyes following every forkful from plate to mouth. They became even more fixated when the selection of local cheeses was uncovered. What is it with dogs and cheese? Teddy started to dribble in expectation and Maisie shifted as close to the table as possible, adopting a Crufts show dog sit while maintaining her pleading look.

It wasn't long before Rob and I were beginning to feel rather full. Dessert was thankfully a fluffy, light as a feather lemony treat, which slid down with little effort, but we'd finally reached that over-stuffed point when it's hard to move, needing to stretch yourself into a very upright posture in an attempt to put more room between the stomach and diaphragm to aid the process of breathing easily.

"That was an awesome meal," said Rob "the food is as good as it always was, but I'm so full I really need to walk some of it off before bed." I couldn't have agreed more.

We gathered up the dirty dishes, placed them back on the tray, and left it outside the room as instructed. We then took the dogs for a lengthy stroll around the dark streets for their final pee before bed. It was damp and cold, but they were happy, having succeeded through their powers of persuasion to profit from a few scraps they forced us to give them at the end of the meal. I swear dogs have mind-altering abilities!

Finding Napoleon!

The next day, our breakfast was taken in our room, our previous night's feast preventing little more than a delicate nibble through a couple of buttery croissants. After glugging several cups of hot, milky coffee, we paid our bill and took a brief drive to a large woodland area on the top of a hill, not far from the hotel, with views over the autumn vineyards. The morning was cold with heavy mist cloaking the area, creating an environment for some wonderful photos. I was in my element taking shots of the vines peeking through the whiteness. Perfectly formed spiders' webs, resembling delicate silver lacework, lay suspended between fence posts and the leafless trees hovered within the mist like ghosts. I left Rob amusing the dogs while I became lost down the lens of my camera for a while.

On this misty morning, the area was deserted, though it could have been because it was early Saturday morning and the locals were enjoying a lie-in and a lazy breakfast. I eventually caught up with Rob on the forest path and together we strolled through the grey mist, the moisture clinging to our warm clothing, our footfalls on the wet leaves refusing to disturb the utter silence. Even the dogs seemed temporarily subdued. Having been here several times before, we knew what we'd find up ahead and it's an extraordinary thing to stumble upon in this particular spot, miles from anywhere noteworthy. It soon came into view, looming out of the mist; an exact replica of the house in which Napoleon Bonaparte was exiled on the island of Elba. As far as we can tell, it serves no purpose other than as a monument to the little French general who faced his nemesis the Duke of Wellington at Waterloo and lost the fight. There is no information board to educate visitors about this structure either and we've always wondered why here, in this unlikely setting? I eventually got around to conducting some research and this is what I discovered:

Captain Claude Noisot was a soldier and captain of the Emperor's guard who retired to Fixin in 1835 He was responsible for creating the park Rob and I were walking in, having bought several hectares of land in the hills and planting Corsican Loricio pine trees in tribute to Napoleon's birthplace. He appeared to be rather obsessed with his Emperor, hence Napoleon's name pops up in several places around the village. Apart from the small Elban house, he commissioned a bronze statue entitled 'Napoléon s'éveillant à l'immortalité', (Napoleon awakes to immortality), created by François Rude, a Dijon sculptor and friend of Noisot.

Leaving the tiny building behind, we climbed a series of small steps carved into the limestone and walked a short way towards this large bronze statue to once more gaze upon the depiction of Napoleon's uniformed corpse, lying semi-prostrate on his side, mostly covered by a large blanket which falls in folds that hover above what appears to be a dead eagle. The title of this sculpture we think is a little ill considered, as Napoleon is portrayed as well and truly deceased and not awake to anything. Maybe a look of surprise or joy on his face might have helped. For the curious among you, you can find images on the internet and see it for yourselves.

As we made our way back to the car, sunlight had begun to pierce the gloom and patches of blue sky were making an appearance. It was going to be a beautiful autumn day, but we, for the most part, would experience little of it as we raced along the *autoroute* to our next overnight stop.

This final night was spent in a pleasant tourist hotel we use a lot. It is reasonably priced and only ten minutes from the tunnel. The restaurant is more canteen than dining room and similar to those found in many hotels of this type, designed to be easily cleaned and satisfy travellers with a standard type meal before they retire to one of the identical rooms, which, in this establishment, are spotlessly clean and have comfortable beds. It also welcomes dogs and on the evening we arrived, half the police force of France. The car park was stuffed with police vehicles. We thought the worst, but only because on a previous visit we witnessed a raid.

The previous autumn, a bright yellow, small and very powerful Mercedes with private UK number plates had captured our attention upon arrival, but only because it stood out like a sore thumb and was parked in the disabled spot next to the entry doors. After settling in, Rob had popped back to reception to ask about dinner and was surprised to see several armed police, one carrying a bag, escorting two handcuffed young Asian men down the stairwell. Our room was directly above the car park and after Rob's return to tell me about it, I was able to see what was happening. The yellow car was being thoroughly searched—windows, doors, boot and bonnet were wide open (trunk and hood if you're an American reading this). Police had it surrounded and were crawling inside and out, with a couple on the floor examining the underneath. Meanwhile, the two men were put into a police car and driven away. We presumed it was drugs related but wondered at the intelligence of the perpetrators whose car stood out like a new moon on a clear night. We would have thought you would want to be as inconspicuous as possible, but what do we know? The most we've ever smuggled was a couple of extra bottles of wine in the days when strict limits applied.

Back to the present. On this occasion, the owners of the police vehicles were not there to arrest anyone, but were populating the conference facilities, no doubt acquiring additional skills; seeking out any Brits who hadn't yet absorbed the new rules since leaving the EU.

The following morning after breakfast, I passed a couple of rather handsome, well-built policemen clad in full uniform, with stab vests and guns in holsters. I bid them *"Bonjour"* and was rewarded with wide smiles and a *"Bonjour Madame"* in return. After climbing into the car, I turned to Rob,

"Did you see those two policemen lounging in reception? Being arrested by them would be quite a thrill." I said, grinning.

"Now that's a good idea. I'll ask them to keep you locked up for a couple of months so I can please myself and not have to worry about you reminding me to put my clothes away, or giving me a telling off for making a mess in the kitchen."

"Can't do that. The dogs would miss me and you'd forget to buy toilet rolls, the consequences of which I'd rather not think about."

PART II

SUMMERTIME TRAVELS

8

Doggie Travel Problems

"It's how much?? Are you kidding me? That's utterly unbelievable! Are you sure? Robbing "&*%%**!!!"

This was Rob's incredulous outburst after I'd just informed him how much it was going to cost to get Teddy and Maisie to France this summer. As we didn't go skiing in February because Covid had resulted in the shutdown of all ski resorts in France, this was the first time we needed to acquire the new Pet Health Certificate, the EU Pet Passport Scheme having ceased at the start of January.

I rang our vet who told me they no longer provided the certificate because it was complicated and took too long to complete. So necessity demanded I trawl around more local vets to see how far I could get. Vet Number One was lovely.

"Yes, we do them for £150 per dog."

I distinctly remember trying hard not to shout "How much!" The shock almost caused me to start hyperventilating and edge towards passing out. I think she heard my sudden intake of breath and went on to say.

"Sorry love, I know they're a lot of money, but they take the vet a long time to complete. It's such a shame for dog owners who have to pay this to take their dogs away on holiday with them, but there's nothing the vet can do about it. We can't help you this time anyway as we've had a rush on them and haven't the time to squeeze any more in."

She kindly recommended another vet a little further afield.

"You might get them a bit cheaper there love," she said. "You never know. Good luck with it."

Leaving the distanced and recommended vet for now, I approached another local practice first, Vet Number Two. Another sympathetic receptionist informed me, after I'd described the amount I'd previously been quoted, they would provide the certificate at a slightly lower rate, but Mrs Head Vet wasn't present until the following day and the receptionist offered to ring me back in the morning. I needed to be patient and await the outcome, living in hope that this vet would oblige.

The next morning I kept my mobile close, but once again, the response was negative.

"I'm sorry, but Mrs Vet won't do them. You're not registered with us and besides, she's had such a bad experience she's refused to go near another."

My interest was piqued and I questioned her further, thinking any knowledge gained could be useful in trying to obtain this gold-plated document for our two pooches. This is what she told me.

"Well" she said. "Mrs Vet completed one for a couple who were going to France with their dog and a few days later, got an irate phone call from them. They were stranded at the Tunnel because a mistake was found on the certificate and the dog wasn't allowed to travel. Mrs Vet was mortified. She had a go at trying to persuade whoever the official was that it was her fault and the dog was fit to travel, but whoever was in charge was having none of it and point blank refused."

I made sympathetic noises and asked what the error had been.

"Dunno, but Mrs Vet is getting on in years, due to retire soon and was forced to meet the couple halfway between here and the Tunnel." At this point, the receptionist started to sound rather upset. "It was a terribly long way to drive and the couple were really angry; not happy at all and quite nasty to Mrs Vet. No need for that is there? She was really upset and stressed and had to drive all the way back. It took her hours. It really tired her out at her age, driving all that way. She's vowed she'll never go near one of those things again, and I don't blame her."

Acknowledging the ordeal was indeed terrible, I finished the call before the receptionist burst into tears at the awfulness of it all.

I was genuinely impressed the vet had agreed to drive a considerable distance to put right this error but was still in the dark about what it was and why she didn't notice it before handing the document over to the owners. I had thought it best not to enquire further before the receptionist totally broke down.

Next on my list was the recommended vet supplied by my first enquiry, incurring a slightly longer journey if an appointment could be agreed upon. Vet Number Three. These proved to be really helpful but explained only one vet at the practice was registered to carry out this task and they needed to ask her personally if she'd do this. She was, apparently, heading to pastures new that very same week. I shamefully resorted to pleading in the hope of gaining some sympathy for my plight. Begging and sounding desperate resulted in a confirmation phone call and an appointment the next day.

In order to facilitate a speedy process, an emailed PDF form arrived containing a request to complete it with Maisie and Teddy's details, as contained on their original passports and to return it immediately. Of course, I obliged as I hoped it would help speed up the process. The following day, we arrived to collect what we presumed to be a simple single-page certificate and couldn't believe the huge wad of A4 pages we were handed, most of which contained meaningless pre-printed gobbledegook more suited to those wishing to transport a lorry load of sheep. Adding insult to injury, the Health Certificate became null and void after one return journey and we would then face this mammoth and expensive farce each time we travelled to France with our dogs. True, this vet had offered the best price to date, but it was still a fortune when compared with the original passports which lasted for several years.

I was further incensed when I discovered all those from countries within the EU could use their 'dog, cat, and ferret' passports to bring their pets into the UK, yet this was not reciprocated. More misery would be faced if wanting to tour around Europe, as a separate Pet Health Certificate is required for each EU country entered. I could have cheerfully strangled the idiot responsible for this particular cock-up in Brexit negotiations!

9

A Day Out For Lunch

Finally back in our Alpes d'Haute Provence, we awoke to a beautiful morning, with a cloudless blue sky and not a breath of air. It was going to be hot and we decided, after several days of not venturing far from the house, to take a trip to Castellane. The town has a very interesting history, with evidence of human civilisations from pre-history. Numerous invasions and sacking of the town occurred throughout the Middle Ages and the seventeenth and eighteenth centuries and I'm pleased that since then, things have settled down. It also lies within the UNESCO Global Geopark, a place we have spent many a happy time with friends and grandchildren searching and finding ammonites. A lovely little museum dedicated to all things geological can be found in the town.

Today, however, geological sea creatures were off the list as we promised ourselves a good lunch in one of the many lively restaurants that appear like magic during the summer months and hoped to find the Saturday market in full swing. Castellane has always been a firm favourite with us and our visitors as it occupies a lovely position on the river Verdon. The river passes under the fifteenth century stone 'Bridge of the Roc', a registered historical site, and proceeds under the modern road bridge heading towards the Gorges du Verdon. The water is crystal clear, washing over rocks and stones creating shallow areas where children can safely enter to play while their parents supervise.

Temperatures can be fierce in the town during the summer months, so spending time sitting on a rock in the middle of the river's flow, dipping your feet into the cool water is a real treat. However, it's not a peaceful experience as you're joined by a chorus of shouting parents, screaming children and barking dogs. We're as guilty as anyone, allowing Maisie and Teddy to leap about in the river, adding to the chaos and noise with their cacophony of delighted barks.

Since the town is the starting point for the drive into the Gorges du Verdon, it is overrun with visitors during July and August and finding a seat at a restaurant during the sacred French lunch break can prove particularly difficult, especially if you want to dine *au plein air*, sitting under a parasol or awning while watching the world go by. It was a blessing we'd arrived a little early for lunch that day as we'd wasted half an hour driving in circles around the town searching for a parking space. We struck lucky when a car vacated a tiny space just as we approached, much to the annoyance of another car trying to get to it first by racing the wrong way around the small car park. I felt very smug as I glanced at the frustrated face of the driver but he looked equally smug when he saw the struggle Rob had getting our huge vehicle into a space that seemed more suited to a Fiat 500!

Nonetheless, we made it in time to wander around the market stalls before they started to pack away, delighting in the variety of Provençal fare on offer. Focussing on the clothes, I resisted any temptation to buy that lovely summer dress I could see decorating the front of the stall. Rob expressed his surprise,

"Wow Jane. You've just managed to resist buying another dress. You sure you're feeling OK?"

I gave him a withering look and decided not to comment.

We had already visited the twice-weekly market in our village, so we had plenty of food supplies back at the house, so our priority now was to find somewhere to relax and enjoy a modest lunch. We wandered across to our usual haunts; a row of restaurants that overlook the square containing the market.

These small premises have most of their seating outside, under brightly coloured canopies with clear sides to give more protection if the weather turns a little inclement or cool. We visit often during the low season when the town has returned to a more tranquil place—the market ceases, the tourist shops are shuttered and most holidaymakers have returned to their normal lives. A table is always available, the staff are more relaxed and have time for a bit of a banter and our dogs benefit from a lot of fuss and attention as they wait to see if any titbits are likely to come their way.

Today though, it was chaos. Every table was taken. Groups of people were standing around on the pavement alongside, hoping that the person they could see nursing a lone coffee might soon be leaving and the table would become free. The staff rushed about, looking red-faced in the heat, with just enough time to deal with anyone asking for a table for four and telling them *"non!"* before rushing off again to take an order or deliver a meal.

We dragged our panting dogs away and headed into the narrow thoroughfare positioned a short walk from the restaurants. Tall buildings on either side kept the street largely in the shade, out of reach of the burning summer sun, making it feel more comfortable. The tourist shops were busy. The ubiquitous lavender, olive and sunflower patterns were everywhere, painted on bright pottery and printed on an array of tableware and linen. Most shops displayed samples of their wares outside, hoping to tempt the browsing public into their interiors. Hats, footwear, clothing, Provençal souvenirs and trinkets were all on show, fighting for space in this tiny street amidst ice cream sellers, bars and a restaurant, plus a shop selling a mishmash of curios. We ignored all enticements to browse or buy as our focus remained on finding somewhere for, what was now, a late lunch.

I was beginning to feel downhearted as everywhere appeared to be full, but we finally found a table at a lovely little restaurant positioned in a tiny side street and happily settled in. While waiting for our meals to be served, we sipped a refreshingly cool rosé wine produced in the vineyards of Provence; a blissful taste of sunshine. Our meals arrived. My creamy wild mushroom risotto was delicious and Rob delighted in his meal of succulent braised lamb in a rich Provençal broth. For dessert, we both chose a slice of *tarte au pommes* served slightly warm, the buttery pastry feather-light, the apples soft and not too sweet. On top, a scoop of vanilla ice cream slowly melting into the apples; the perfect end to the meal.

Replete and thoroughly content, we sat back sipping small cups of expresso while watching a little child playing with a ball in the street. A beady-eyed Teddy, who had been lying quietly under the table, spotted a chance for some playtime skulduggery. All thoughts of relaxation were abandoned as Rob was forced to grab Teddy's lead, hanging on for dear life as our excited dog started to hurtle like a missile towards the ball. After avoiding the embarrassment of being dragged out of his chair by our madcap hound, he succeeded in hauling a very reluctant Teddy back to a position next to the table, accompanied by a stern telling off that Teddy simply shrugged off.

At this point, I have to tell you that Teddy, our rescued Fox Terrier, has a passion for chasing balls and is a past master at locating them. He is forever disappearing into the undergrowth to return a few minutes later with a ball in his mouth. He's not fussy either as anything related to a ball is fair prey, happily emerging from a dense hedgerow having sought out a burst football, half a tennis ball or a scrap of rubber that was once part of one. Of course, we attempt to prise these rather unhygienic items from his jaws, but trying to dislodge from his mouth what is now slimy with saliva is like trying to extract egg white from a basin with your fingers and basins don't have teeth!

There have also been occasions when an unsuspecting owner throwing a ball for his own dog, has had to put up with our sharp-eyed Teddy launching like a greyhound out of the blocks and speeding after it. If he reaches it first, he takes full possession. The other dog is now confused and usually gives up, believing his owner was pulling a fast one by stuffing the ball into his pocket instead. Patience is needed at this point while Teddy is having a whale of a time, gallivanting around the park tossing the ball in the air, with Maisie haring after him barking non-stop. He will eventually return and drop it at our feet, begging one of us to throw it. We throw his own ball instead and return the stolen one, now rather soggy, back to the rightful owner with a grovelling apology. Thankfully, most owners take it all in their stride, as often, their dogs can be ball thieves too.

A Bit of Bell Ringing

As we left Castellane behind us, it remained hot and sunny as we drove steadily up the twisting road that heads away from the town towards the southern end of Lac Castillon. The jumble of Castellane's rooftops had disappeared from view, but the *Chapel of Our Lady,* perched atop the *Rock of Notre Dame,* could still be seen; a beacon of faith to those who believe its dominating position at 184 metres (604 feet) above the town is closer to heaven.

One autumn several years ago, Rob and I tackled the steep climb up to the small chapel, rebuilt three times since its original construction in the twelfth century. Once at the top, we found the view over Castellane towards the far distant hills was breathtaking, especially as it was awash with autumn colour against a slab of blue sky. The chapel was open and I located a long rope hanging by the main door.

"Go on," said Rob. "Pull it. I dare you." So with no-one around, I did, just once, sending the sound of the bell echoing across the rooftops below. I just hoped it wasn't some kind of warning, imagining folk tumbling out of their homes and rushing towards the nearest point of safety, but the population remained calm, going about their business undisturbed, no doubt wondering about the idiot who had chosen to temporarily disturb the peace. With the bell stilled, quiet returned to our spot high above the town, the only sound being bird song and the autumn leaves rustling in the breeze.

10

Car Trouble

We arrived at the lake to find it packed with people on pedallos, kayaks and paddle boards. The beach area was awash with tables, chairs and bright parasols, with a large van conveniently positioned beside the footpath, serving hot food, ice creams and drinks. We had both dogs on the lead to prevent any catastrophes linked to balls and followed a familiar pathway that led us to a more secluded spot. Here, if in the water, there appeared less risk of being hit by a wayward pedalo. Both dogs were anxious for a swim, desperate to cool off as the heat had been intense.

Under a sunny sky, the bright turquoise waters sat amidst tall hills covered in umbrella pines and deciduous trees in full leaf. Behind, the hills rolled towards the north end of the lake, eight kilometres away, gradually gaining height as they marched onwards, finally evolving into the mountains visible in the distance. Opposite, the road we would take later, tracked the meanders created by the water, hugging the hillsides as it progressed over the 100 metre high dam (328 feet) and continued on its way.

The area at this southern end of the lake is crisscrossed by small footpaths through the trees and scrub, some ending at accessible inlets, others winding their way through the hinterland where you may stumble across a derelict building, the sad remains of what appears to have been a restaurant; isolated, covered in graffiti and encroached upon by Mother Nature. It possibly served the village of Castillon, itself no longer existing, sacrificed to the waters and resting 25-30 metres (82-98 feet)deep under the lake's surface after being dynamited to make room for construction of the dam.

Back at the end of the nineteenth century the idea of creating Lac Castillon was born. A need for drinking water and irrigation was the main purpose for the lake's creation. The two world wars were the cause of interruptions to the building work, but after liberation in 1945, over two thousand workers, including eight hundred German prisoners of war, pushed construction to completion in 1948. The lake finally reached its maximum depth in July 1949.

A curiosity we've often wondered about, concerns the ruins of a settlement, resting high above the lake. On many occasions we have wandered along a footpath with friends or family to explore this long abandoned place and take images of the stunning views over Lac Castillon's blue waters. We initially believed it to be part of the village of Castillon, but research finally revealed the ruined castle and its church date from medieval times and were part of the small commune of Demandolx which still exists today a short distance away.

We visit the south end of the lake often and generally find it peaceful, devoid of human activity apart from the odd walker or two, with or without a dog for company. However, it was the time of year when all of Europe is on holiday. Peace and quiet had summered elsewhere as the place resonated with the babble created by hordes of holidaymakers having a great time. Above the shrieks and general hubbub, a sudden and distant rumble of thunder focused my attention on a darkening sky which appeared to be heading our way. A few drops of light rain heralded what was likely to be a heavy downpour.

"Quick, get the dogs out of the water before we get soaked." I shouted. Both dogs were called. Maisie arrived beside us, shaking the water from her fur, soaking us in the process. Teddy had other ideas and remained "doggie paddling" around in circles, just out of reach.

"You'll have to go in and get him. I can't because I've got my trainers and socks on", said Rob as he was placing Maisie on the lead.

"What do you think these are then?" I responded pointing to my sandals, "flippin' waders?"

"I know, but you can get them off more easily than me!" he reasoned.

"Oh for heaven's sake, give me the lead."

Marching towards the lake edge, I grabbed a stick and hurled it towards our aquatic dog. "Playtime", thought Teddy, who promptly grabbed the stick in his mouth and swam to shore, dropping it at my feet. He's an intelligent and mischievous boy and now on dry land, he intuited my intention to put him back on his lead, so remained just out of reach. When he's like this, lunging at him never works. He just moves away, challenging us with a fixed stare. However, we've learned over time that a stick is a much yearned-for object and he simply can't resist the urge to retrieve one. Waving it in front of his nose achieved the desired result as he grabbed it in his jaws and proceeded to play a game of tug that nearly pulled my arm from its socket. Seconds later, with my free hand, I seized his harness and Teddy was once more on his lead, staring longingly at the stick which, after its release, was thrown into the lake and was now floating away into the distance.

Another clap of thunder, louder this time, reminded us it was time to get a move on. As we passed by the beach area, people were rushing to pack away their belongings and, like us, heading for their cars. A few hardy souls remained splashing about in the water. Wet dogs loaded, we headed off, leaving the storm in our wake. Inside the car, as light rain began to fall, we comfortably settled in for the forty-minute drive. The dogs were snuggled on the back seat, snoozing and drying off. All was well.

Twenty minutes later, all was not well. Crossing a narrow bridge over the river, the car delivered a thumping noise, followed by a heavy grating sound which set my teeth on edge. The car rolled forward and I began to panic.

"What the hell was that?" Did we hit something? Is it under the car?"

The engine revved as Rob tried to get the car moving. "It's not going anywhere. It won't drive at all." he said, glumly.

Thankfully, the car had rolled far enough for Rob to guide it onto a patch of dirt alongside the road and off the bridge. I sat stupefied while Rob looked around our knackered vehicle to see if he could find the problem. Arriving back in the present I joined him on the roadside, returning across the bridge, gathering up large, oily ball bearings that were scattered in the road at various points. It was decided the problem was a drive shaft. (For those interested, it was discovered later the Constant Velocity Joint had broken, whatever one of those is). A rumble of thunder announced that the storm had chased us along the valley and was closing in. With tall mountains around us, it was impossible to see just how far away it was. We retired to the car to argue.

Rob: "Where's the insurance document?"

Me: "What makes you think I've got it? You arranged it."

Rob "Yes, and I printed it off and gave it to you to go in the car."

Me: "You never told me to put it in the car."

Rob: "So where the hell is it then?"

Me: "It's in the wallet file with all the other paperwork we needed for this holiday."

Rob: "Where's the file."

Me: "Back at the house."

Rob: "What! Didn't you think to put it in the car for heaven's sake?"

Me: "No, so why didn't you do it then Mr 'It's never my fault'."

Rob: "No, this isn't my fault, it's yours!"

Me: "How's that then? Thought the car had been thoroughly serviced before we left anyway."

Rob: "You know it was. The only mention was a small tear in the gator."

Me: "See! It is your fault. You should have had it repaired!"

The bickering continued, while unnoticed, the storm moved closer. A loud rumble of thunder reminded us we needed to stop behaving like children and DO SOMETHING!

Here's a résumé of what happened next.

Rob had forgotten the insurance company name. I blame his age. Rob rings our son at home in the UK.

Son contacts us to say he's found the company name and number, informing us they will ring in five minutes.

Mobile rings. Rob explains the situation to the operator.

Operator asks for our location. We tell him. He asks us to spell it as he doesn't know how to spell French names, was new to the job and this was his first ever call. Trust us to land a 'newbie'.

Rob's phone only has seven percent of signal left. He spells out the name of the bridge and location … three times … slowly.

Rob tells the novice operator his phone signal is depleting rapidly and gives him my mobile number, just in case.

A rapidly darkening sky, a rumble of thunder and a flash of lightning. A storm is approaching.

After a few minutes, the novice rings back. He thinks he's found where we are, but can't pronounce it, so spells it out, slowly.

I'm panicking at Rob's rapidly depleting signal and wanted to scream at the nice, but oh-so-slow novice operator to GET A BLOODY MOVE ON!

The novice then excels himself by asking if we can use Google to locate a garage nearby that might be able to fix a Landrover and give them a ring. We're in the middle of nowhere, in the mountains and it's Saturday evening. Is he mad? He rings off to speak to his manager. Rob's phone is almost at zero.

I spend several minutes on my phone searching needlessly for a garage just in case failure to do so will nullify the insurance because it 'states it in the small print'. My phone signal is now dangerously low.

The novice rings Rob back. His manager is on the case and will be in touch in fifteen minutes or so.

I walk the dogs down by the river under a darkening sky. When I return, the manager has called Rob's mobile and explained a breakdown truck will be with us in twenty minutes and then a taxi will arrive to take us to the house, but he needs confirmation of our Tunnel reservation to prove we are who we say we are. Rob's mobile dies.

The signal on my mobile is coming and going due to the storm. I find the confirmation on my phone and send it off just as the signal completely disappears.

Loud thunder and light rain.

The breakdown truck duly arrives. I remove dogs and other paraphernalia from the rear of the car and stand in the mud just off the roadway watching as the car is dragged onto the truck. Rob signs a document. The truck moves off, the driver waving as he passes my pathetic figure shivering at the side of the road, looking like a refugee. Then it starts to rain heavily.

The storm arrives overhead. The thunder deafening as it bounces off the mountains and echoes along the valley. The lightning is almost constant, slashing across the slate-grey sky every couple of seconds. The rain is torrential, so much so that it is hard to see. It's like being in Hades.

Ten minutes pass. Where is that damn taxi!

Then the hail arrives, thumping down in vicious, stinging bits of ice. Rob has my little telescopic umbrella which proves useless in these conditions. I have a large golf brolly. We're in shorts and tee shirts. It's freezing!

Another ten minutes. Still no taxi.

The dogs are shivering, so I lean down and shelter them with the brolly leaving most of me exposed to the elements. I'm soaked and shivering violently and we're all now standing in a rivulet of water that appeared from nowhere and was rapidly getting deeper.

The hail retreats to be replaced by heavy rain once more as the storm continues to rage overhead.

Two or three cars pass. None of them is the promised taxi and none of them stops to help. I feel like crying.

The storm eventually starts to drift away, it's getting dark and it's still raining.

An ambulance approaches, pulls in and two male paramedics get out asking, '*Êtes-vous OK*?" I'm in awe. We are being rescued by a couple of angels in paramedic uniforms who quickly load our sodden troupe into their immaculately clean vehicle.

Rob and one paramedic sit in the back, occupying the empty patient bed; the dogs are on the floor with our detritus and soggy brollies. I'm up front with the driver to provide him with directions.

Twenty minutes later we are back in our house. We thank the

paramedics profusely. I want to hug them, but presume the last thing they'd want is a bedraggled, rain-soaked English woman invading their personal space. I attempt a photo of them and their ambulance, forgetting my mobile has died, so you'll have to take my word for it!

Later the dogs, after being towel dried and fed, were asleep on the sofa. Rob and I were no longer suffering from hyperthermia having enjoyed a hot shower each and a good old cuppa, the British cure for everything. Later, after snacking on anything we could get our hands on, we sat curled up next to the dogs, nursing a glass of wine, mulling over the day's event and baulking at the thought of the next stage in this saga.

11

There's Nothing Wrong with Camping

I neglected to tell you that our Discovery had a roof box containing a load of camping gear, in fact, ALL our camping gear. We spent many a year camping throughout France when our children were small and somehow have never broken the habit of enjoying time sleeping on the floor with what is, in effect, a sheet of nylon protecting us from the elements. Things have improved considerably since those holidays spent under heavy canvas, attempting to get comfortable on an inflatable and very bouncy mattress which creaked every time we moved. One of the benefits of clever people who spend time developing such things is that camping nowadays is easier and more comfortable, though I know most of our friends totally disagree with this.

I admit that many people may dislike the idea of camping because of what they see are major drawbacks, such as sharing toileting and washing facilities with total strangers, but it's not that bad. Honest. These days it tends to be all private cubicles with lockable doors as long as you choose modern sites and not *'camping a la ferme'* where you may find yourself sharing an earth loo and a grubby basin in a barn filled with cows. Washing up in most 'posh' sites becomes a social occasion, chatting to the person at the next sink who is keen to practise their English. *"You is Engleeesh? Ou est you live in Angleterre? I been London."* Often these bilingual chats continue whenever you bump into each other around the site, which sometimes results in an invite to share a glass or three. *"You come ce soir pour une leetle verre de vin, yes?"*

The most important thing is your pitch and the distance it is from the 'conveniences'. Too far and your walk, when desperate, can be taxing and nothing is worse than standing in your shower cubicle, naked and realising you've left something vital behind in the tent, like your towel or a clean pair of knickers. This is something you only do once and after this initial *faux pas*, you'll never forget again for the duration of your stay. Believe me. I speak from experience! If your pitch is too near the facilities, you'll have people traipsing past your tent at all hours and be kept awake by the sound of flushing toilets.

I admit we'd not camped for years, but succumbed to spending a fortune on modern gear in 2020 in order to try and capture some of the excitement of life in the great outdoors, choosing beautiful locations where, most importantly, it would be dry, sunny and warm!

When we told people we intended to go camping again we faced ridicule. "What? At your age?" It's surprising just how many folk still think camping means crawling into a small A-frame tent in the middle of a boggy field. We attempt to debunk this notion, pointing out we're not part of a scouting troupe on a field trip and actually have access to electricity, an induction hob and even a carpet! I kid you not, it came with the tent. Our enthusiastic explanations usually land on deaf ears, no matter how we dress it up. It seems camping is very much a 'marmite' thing. (*Marmite is a thick, gluey beef extract paste that people either love or hate.*)

With our lovely little Les Hirondelles sitting as it does in beautiful Haute Provence, we made the decision to spend one week away camping each time we venture there during the summer. As we stay for at least four weeks nowadays, we can afford the time to travel further afield. On this trip, we had set our sights on the Hérault department, a place we'd never visited, except to race through on our way to somewhere else. From research, it appeared to have plenty of interesting places to visit in beautiful settings. We'd booked a pitch (*emplacement*) on a four-star 'eco' site, set on the banks of the river Hérault. Our arrival there was expected in two days' time, but we were now *sans voiture* and *sans tente*.

12

Car Hire Troubles and a Train Journey

T he morning after the trip to Hell the previous afternoon, the insurance company called to inform us the Discovery had been taken to a garage in a village we know well, on the route down to Nice. They also told us they had kindly arranged a hire car, *"une compact voiture, très economique monsieur."* It was waiting for us in Marseille. There were several things wrong with this. To reach Marseille without the use of a car was problematic. Using public transport would be long and complicated. Using a taxi for the entire journey would leave us destitute after paying the fare. The *compact voiture* would be just big enough to squeeze in the two of us and the dogs, with my handbag filling the boot space!

Rob patiently explained we needed a car big enough to take our camping gear, our luggage, two dogs and ourselves. We also needed it the day after tomorrow.

The second call came. They'd found us a large people carrier, once again in Marseille. Apparently, we could only have it for three days as it was booked for someone else. We would have to return it to Marseille and pick up another car. We digested the information, calmly, with a frisson of total disbelief considering we had explained our requirements prior to this current call.

Getting from the house to Marseille involved a two-hour train journey to Nice with an onward train taking a further three hours on a good day. In the middle of August, we were informed it could be longer. After paying around sixty euros each in fares and taking three hours to drive back, we then had no choice but to drive to the garage in charge of repairing the car to retrieve our camping gear. Add in the time we'd spend hanging about dealing with paperwork, it was well over twelve hours. We'd also face the whole thing again in reverse as well as a day's interruption to our camping break as we changed the car for another. I could feel myself getting stressed and wished we lived in fantasy land where we had access to dear old Scottie at the controls of his transporter on the Star Ship Enterprise!

I could hear the frustration in Rob's voice as he explained why this was madness and unrealistic. He asked the operator what was wrong with the car hire at Nice Airport, two hours away. We could get there with only one train journey. A pregnant pause followed while the operator mulled this over and obviously wondered why he hadn't thought of it in the first place. Weird when you consider Nice Airport has just about every car hire company on the planet. A few hours later, another call from the insurance company confirmed a Citroen C5 had been secured for us to collect the following day. Being a bit of a worry guts, I said to Rob "What's one of those? Is it big enough for everything? What are we going to do if it isn't?"

Rob rolled his eyes. "It'll be fine. Quit worrying. It'll be a bit of a squeeze, but it's just about large enough to take the whole shebang."

Gilbert offered to drive the two of us down the valley to the tiny station that serves the wonderful *Train de Pigne*, (the Pine Cone Train), which runs between Nice and Dignes les Bains, the capital of Haute Provence. We asked if he'd be willing to take the dogs for a short walk around midday as we had no choice but to leave them in the house while we undertook the journey, meaning they would be alone for hours. With his usual willingness to help out, *"Pas de tout.* Not at all," he said.

It's a delightful journey as the train trundles the 94 miles (157 km) along its narrow gauge railway line. The construction started in 1890 and took twenty-one years to complete. Hardly surprising when you consider the terrain it faced, meandering through the mountains, crossing rivers and following routes through valleys, necessitating the building of viaducts, bridges and the creation of twenty-seven tunnels. The Tunnel de la Colle St Michel, just outside our local station, is the longest on the route and stretches 2.5 miles (just over 4 kilometres), punching through the mountains separating the Var valley from the upper Verdon valley. It's an amazing achievement considering it was accomplished with only manpower, dynamite and shovels.

Travelling on this little train isn't a speedy experience. The journey takes a couple of hours between our local station and Nice, about the same duration as the journey by car, but far more pleasurable. The train will stop occasionally to pick up a passenger or two who are waiting at something akin to a bus stop. Small stations, no more than a platform and a couple of tiny buildings, pepper the route alongside the villages they serve. However, speed isn't important as you relax and watch the stunning scenery slide by your window, added to the knowledge you've avoided the stresses of negotiating the Niçoise traffic. With the advent of the superb tram service in Nice, there is also no need to face the extortionate cost of a taxi to or from the airport either.

Gilbert knocked on the door bright and early the following morning and delivered us to the station in time for our train which arrived dead on time. Settling into our comfortable seats, with the early morning sun streaming through the windows, we were looking forward to our trip, but it didn't quite go to plan ...

The train proceeded over the viaduct that crosses the river Verdon and entered the darkness of the St Michel tunnel before emerging once again into bright sunshine. The first mandatory stop was the picture postcard village of Méailles, perched atop an escarpment and teetering on the edge of the cliff face, its pale ochre houses and russet tiled roofs set against a backdrop of green fields that gradually merge into the tree-clad lower slopes of the mountains. As the train slowly entered the station positioned at the foot of the cliff, we glimpsed the steep and twisting pathway that snakes upwards towards the village. That morning it appeared the residents were not in the mood for strenuous exercise as the train pulled out without any changes in passenger numbers. It pressed on and didn't stop at the two optional waiting points as no-one was hanging around to hail it. The tiny village of Fugeret presented no passengers either so our little train rumbled onwards towards its next stop.

Annot is a tourist village running along the foot of the famous sandstones and nestled beneath 100 year-old Chestnut trees. The village receives copious amounts of visitors throughout the year looking to hike amidst the stones, stroll through the shade of the trees or to wander through the medieval streets. It is also the place where the truly dramatic scenery ends as the land begins to tumble, bit by bit, from sky to sea. In our case, the train journey ended too as we were all ushered from the carriages and onto a coach. Surprisingly, everyone accepted this without complaint, presuming that something was amiss further along the line. Our journey progressed by road, dropping people off at various points until the coach pulled up and we were ushered back onto the train for the final leg into Nice.

The trams ensured the remainder of our journey out to the airport was straightforward, and we found the hire car ready and waiting. A couple of hours later we pulled into the garage responsible for repairing our Discovery and explained we needed to retrieve our camping gear. After kindly offering us a step ladder to reach the top box, Rob began emptying the contents, handing them to me waiting below. The pile grew steadily.

"OK. That's it," said Rob, "the top box is empty."

"Where's the new sleeping bag?

"That's it there." Rob said, pointing towards the huge pile of camping detritus resting on the tarmac.

"No, it isn't. That's not the new one, I bought that a few months ago. The new one is red."

"Are you sure?"

"Yes. I put it with all the rest of the camping stuff in the cupboard at home, so why didn't you pack it?"

"It couldn't have been in the cupboard because I emptied it all out. You must have put it somewhere else."

"No, I didn't! I bet you've left it behind. For heaven's sake, we've now got one single sleeping bag between us because you forgot the other." I countered, voice raising a couple of decibels.

Rob looked sheepish. "Sorry aren't I? No need to go over the top. It's not the end of the world. I'm sure we can manage with one. I doubt I'll need it anyway. I'll be too hot."

"Yeah, right."

The 'red' one was discovered when we arrived back home in the UK. "Told you so." I said, smugly!

13

The Herault

Postcard One: Our Eco Site

The following morning, with the Citroen packed to the gunnels, we headed off for our week in the Hérault sunshine. It wasn't a particularly auspicious start as it poured with rain for the entire journey, stopping just before we arrived at the site with the sun making a brief appearance before it slipped below the lofty hilltops.

As I mentioned earlier, the site was classified as 'eco-friendly'. It extended across multiple acres, with swathes of green areas and trees, positioned in the centre of extensive vines backed by rolling hills. It was a gorgeous spot. We were given a large pitch a stone's throw from the river, the sound of its rushing waters providing a soothing backdrop. With electricity, water, a picnic table and benches, plus a great position with regard to the facilities, we were delighted. With so much room, pitches were well spaced and Rob was thrilled to discover a communal BBQ area. At this juncture, I should mention that Rob loves to BBQ and I often struggle to temper his enthusiasm if he suggests cooking a BBQ meal when it's minus one outside or pouring with rain. Must be a man thing ... though I'm aware that this isn't always the case. The site was owned and run by the family who produced organic wine from the surrounding vineyards, though, it being very expensive, we shopped for our own wine which we kept cool in the full-sized fridge we'd rented from the site at the time of booking.

The domain had earned its eco-responsible *Clef Verte* (Green Key) label through being conscientious about its environmental impact; ensuring waste is sorted, avoiding all plastics, installing water consumption reducers, managing energy and ensuring no chemicals are used on the 115 hectares (284 acres) of the domain. Even the food served in the restaurant originated from sustainable organic sources. The pool used fresh water with no added chlorine. This came from a natural source, though exactly where this was located remained a mystery.

The non-use of chemicals in the pool was no doubt a noble cause, but there was a downside. When we were there, the water was a dark green. Negotiating the stone entry steps revealed a slimy, slippery coating of algae under your feet which continued along the entire bottom. Everyone seemed to manage and the pool remained fairly busy, but most people it seemed, preferred to spend the day on the banks of the river Hérault. The water was lovely and clean and varied between shallow fast-flowing sections, deep pools and stony banks allowing for the safe crossing on foot to the other side. Children were delighted at being able to use inflatables safely, dogs enjoyed scampering in and out of the water and adults could swim or relax depending on their mood. The flotillas of kayaks, originating from a multitude of rental establishments further upstream, appeared the only drawback. I admit the kayaking looked like great fun, but the sheer amount of them floating past became a bit of an aggravation, requiring eyes in the back of your head to ensure you didn't end up colliding with one.

Postcard Two: Plans, Struggles and Giggles

We'd chosen the Hérault for the reasons previously mentioned and were looking forward to exploring the area. I'd done a fair bit of research before leaving home, but the campsite reception provided a very helpful leaflet detailing the 'must-sees'. That first morning, we threw back our single sleeping bag which had been unzipped and used as a bed cover, and attempted to get up. Our self-inflating memory foam mattress, approximately four inches thick (10 cm), came highly recommended. True to the advertising bumph, it was surprisingly comfortable and issued no unpleasant noises when one of us moved. However, there appeared to be no instruction aimed at old fossils like us about the impossibility of actually getting up from it. We avoid flapping around like a pair of beached whales by manoeuvring onto our knees before standing. If your knees are past their sell-by date, then being well-practised in yoga is advised. Maybe a 'downward dog', just as long as you can balance while you walk your hands towards your feet and stand without crashing onto your bum or falling forwards to perform a face plant! Thankfully we manage the process with some degree of decorum, though we often collapse in giggles at the comedy of it all. As a final warning, if you need to get up during the night, you might be guilty of causing a bit of rumpus as you topple over your sleeping partner in the dark, who won't be pleased with being trampled upon in the early hours.

Rob: "Ouch. Ouch! OUCH! What the bloody hell are you doing? Gerroff! Think my arm's broken."

Me: "Shush! You'll wake up the campsite and stop exaggerating, your arm's fine. Where's the torch? I need a wee."

Rob: "Why in God's name didn't you go before we came to bed?"

Me: "Because I didn't want to go then, did I."

Rob: "You can be a real pain sometimes, you know that?"

Me: "Oh shut up and go back to sleep."

Postcard Three: Exploring Ganges and Laroque

Our first day consisted of a trip into the busy town of Ganges. We needed that sleeping bag and provisions. Food and drink were easy but trying to find a sports shop that sold camping gear meant driving around Ganges in circles, becoming very familiar with the town but failing to find suitable premises. We resorted to asking Mr Google who proved to be extremely familiar with our whereabouts and politely showed us the way. One new sleeping bag later, heading back towards the campsite, we stopped in the little village of Laroque. The idea of lunch beside the river was immediately appealing, as several restaurants had set up trade under a lengthy awning at the side of the through road. This meant all meals and drinks were ferried from the doorways on the opposite side. I was happy the serving staff managed to avoid being hit by a speeding car as they negotiated their way across laden with plates of food. The restaurants sat high above the river, busy with the ubiquitous kayaks and canoes, most of which became stuck on the top of the concrete weir. Watching the occupants trying to dislodge them proved to be an amusing distraction for the diners. Most kayakers succeeded, but if the heaviest occupant was positioned in the back of a canoe, it was a different story and their antics resulted in some very funny moments.

One particular canoe contained an extremely large male at the rear, leaving his small friend to thrust the vessel forwards, obviously getting nowhere. His large companion joined in, but he was so heavy, the back of the canoe was tilted lower into the water. Eventually, the penny dropped. They were going to swap places, carefully removing themselves into the water in order to negotiate past one another. Much to the delight of the viewing public, it didn't go quite to plan. The canoe capsized and the fast flowing water and slippery river bed was making life difficult as they stumbled around, each falling into the shallow water on a regular basis, while trying to cling onto their canoe, now trying to make a run for it on its own. Food was going cold as diners watched on, cheering and shouting at the unfortunates below. Finally, with the canoe right side up, our two victims belly flopped like seals into their seats, risking another capsize as they manoeuvred themselves into the correct position. The canoe wobbled dangerously and the audience held its breath, hoping this comedy of errors would continue. Placing the paddles across their laps, they gradually forced themselves forwards and the canoe slid over the wear to much applause, rapidly turning into loud laughter as the canoe swerved towards the bank and capsized once more.

"We'll have to eat here again," said Rob. "The entertainment is great!"

We took the opportunity after lunch to walk off some of the excesses and explore. Like many French villages, it consisted of old houses with pretty window boxes or pots filled with bright flowers. The streets were narrow and eventually led us towards a church beyond which lay a few more homes before the countryside intruded and stretched away into the distance. It was a peaceful and pretty spot, but there was nothing to really hold our attention for long, so, with the dogs trotting happily by our side, we headed back to the car.

That evening, as the sun was slowly setting, we enjoyed a lengthy stroll around the perimeter of the domain, passing by vines and wandering along the banks of the river to arrive back at our pitch. As darkness descended, with surrounding tents and awnings lit by a celebration of string lights or lanterns, we settled down with a welcome glass of wine. With the dogs dozing at our feet, we discussed where our explorations would take us next and, more seriously, our sleeping arrangements now we had two sleeping bags; should we use one each, or unzip both, sleeping on one and using the other as a coverlet? We chose the latter until I woke up feeling chilled the following morning, devoid of cover as Rob had dragged the entire thing off me.

Postcard Four: The Cascade de la Vis

Our first of the recommended visits was to the Cascade de la Vis. It was ridiculously busy when we arrived, with parking impossible as the whole area was stuffed with vehicles and people crowding the roads as they made their way to and from the falls. We eventually squeezed the Citroen into a tiny space, restricting the already narrow road further. I had to be quick if I was to capture the cascade on camera before we were the cause of traffic chaos. Carefully picking my way along a steep and narrow path between the trees, I found myself in the perfect spot.

The river Vis flowed within a steep-sided valley. Dense vegetation hugged both sides with the falls stretching the entire width of the river, forming a perfect crescent. The water looked calm approaching the rim but turned into a raging torrent as it plunged over the edge creating a fine spray with those near enough benefiting from its cooling effect as they lay toasting under a blazing sun. Away from the base of the falls, youngsters were throwing themselves into the clear water from the smooth rocks on either side, shouting encouragement to their friends to do the same. It was a joyful, if noisy and crowded scene. The falls themselves were truly lovely and I was happy we'd visited, but selfishly wished everyone else had stayed at home!

Postcard Five: Cirque de Navacelles

Rob and I had never heard of the *Cirque de Navacelles*. The tiny image in the campsite information brochure didn't give much away, but what we could see looked interesting, so off we went, passing the waterfall en route, following the course of the river Vis through the valley. It wasn't long before the river disappeared from view as the road started to climb steeply around a multitude of bends, eventually levelling out. Leaving behind the lush greenery in the valley below, we now found ourselves surrounded by a flat, arid landscape which turned out to be part of the *Causses de Blandas and Larzac* in the heart of the *Cévennes National Park*. It appeared quite bleak and desolate, but a welcoming hostelry eventually came into view. Pulling into the car park and finding it full, we resorted to abandoning the car 500 metres away on the roadside verge. Notices on the side of the building informed us a *point de vue* was located at the rear. We sauntered through the café area, emerging onto a paved terrace where visitors could sit and enjoy a coffee or snack, but it was the view we'd come to see and it turned out to be quite something.

The Cirque was extraordinary and we'd never seen anything quite like it. At 300 metres deep (984 ft), this enormous bowl-shaped canyon, unique in Europe, lay beneath our feet, the sinuous route down etched into the steep sides. Looking like miniature toys, the houses forming the tiny hamlet of Navacelles could be seen nestled at the bottom, squeezed into two separate areas at the farthest point. Away from the hamlet, a mini mountain of rock we later found to be called the *Rocher de la Vierge* or 'Oyster Rock' rose up from the base, surrounded by a sea of greenery.

We decided to journey down, but not before we'd had a drink and a snack, so settled ourselves at a small table at the front of the building to enjoy our sandwiches and coffee. Suddenly, peace and tranquillity were rudely interrupted, disturbed by a raucous tirade. A quick glance around failed to reveal the guilty party. There followed an earth-shattering screech. Rob and I looked at one another wondering whether someone was being attacked, hidden out of sight around the side of the main building. My curiosity, combined with the need for a wee, sent me scurrying towards the toilets hoping I wasn't forced to engage in fisticuffs with an assailant on the way.

The source of the noise eyed me steadily as I approached, safely imprisoned behind the bars of his cage. He let out another ear-splitting screech and proceeded to offer a few unintelligible words before hopping over to scrutinise me more closely. Mr Parrot was scrupulous in his examination, cocking his head to one side, finally concluding I was harmless. We made friends, but he appeared to be rather put out when he haughtily rejected my attempts to persuade him to say 'hello' in English. He also refused to say 'goodbye' upon my return journey, obviously wondering what I was going on about before loudly showing his disapproval with a final screech and fluffing of feathers. I reported back to Rob while Mr Parrot continued to exercise his vocal cords.

It had been quite a surprise to see a Parrot shoved into a small spot outside the toilet building, but surmised he was a little too keen on the sound of his own voice to be allowed into a more public space and, more seriously, was probably guilty of hurling insults at unsuspecting tourists.

Leaving our avian friend to his squawking, we found the road down to Navacelles wasn't as scary as it appeared after choosing to drive rather than take the shuttle bus. We easily found a parking space and continued our exploration on foot. Following a pathway, we arrived at the spot where the youthful river Vis flowed gently under an arched mule bridge. This pretty bridge was constructed in 1595 and used to transport animals, humans and goods across the river. Constructed from local stone with a tall arch, it has been able to avoid any floods and remains as an authentic reminder of the past. Today, the narrow pathway is used by tourists and hikers who wish to follow the winding trails on the opposite side.

Flowing beneath, the shaded waters were shallow and crystal clear and our dogs were able to quench their thirst and enjoy a cooling paddle. The river then continued under the shade of the trees to tumble down the rocks and boulders forming a beautiful eight metre high waterfall. It was this river that created the Cirque, cutting a meandering route through the limestone, eventually abandoning its old river bed and finding a more direct route. We could see why the Cirque was listed as a UNESCO world heritage site and were thrilled we'd had the opportunity to visit but left wondering how the tiny population of this isolated hamlet survived when summer became a distant memory and bad weather began to intrude.

Postcard Six: Marcheé de la Poterie

The gorges of the Hérault River were our last recommended visit and once again we passed through some stunning bucolic scenery. The gorges themselves were heaving with traffic and visitors. Not wishing to waste time searching for parking or fighting the crowds, we decided to continue on, missing out on the more dramatic scenery where the river flows through some steep-sided cuttings as it heads towards the Devil's Bridge. With many precipitous gorges surrounding us in Haute Provence, we didn't feel too bad about giving this one a miss.

Our surprise of the day materialised in the shape of a young lady in a 'high vis' vest guarding a notice saying *Route Barée* (road closed).

We'd been hoping to find a venue for lunch in a village we'd spied from the main road but instead had tumbled across a market. The young lady in question directed us towards a large area of land being used as a temporary car park and as the day was baking hot and sunny, we secured a shady parking spot under a large tree.

With the dogs in tow, we approached the entrance to the village, passing under a stone archway into a large open square. A couple of restaurants busy with diners seated under coloured awnings populated one side, with the middle of the square occupied by a *Marcheé de la Poterie*. Presented with stalls displaying beautiful examples of high-quality artisan pottery, a pleasant half an hour or so was spent browsing and I fell in love with several pieces, but they were sadly well out of our price range. Putting all thoughts of maxing out the credit cards aside, the aroma of cooked food from the nearby restaurants reminded us we were starving. A simple lunch of pizza and a cooling glass of beer was ordered, devoured and enjoyed. The dogs didn't miss out either after receiving a bowl of water from the waiter and several pieces of leftover pizza crust that Rob craftily fed to them while they patiently waited under the table.

All good things come to an end and our week in the Hérault had flown by. We'd discovered yet another intriguing part of France, so different to the dramatic scenery we were used to in the Alpes d'Haute Provence, but beautiful nonetheless as it basks in an array of varied and picturesque scenery. Our drive back was miraculously achieved without any accidents or breakdowns, the weather remained kind and of course, we bought Gilbert and Annie some of the terrain's wine and the area's award-winning cheese as a thank you for being the perfect neighbours.

14

Philippe, His Mates and a Motorbike

T hings had still not improved with regard to mobile phone signals at our spot on the mountain, even though we can see the mast nestled within the pines opposite on the route to the Colle de St Michel. Getting a signal inside the house is a bit hit and miss but will sometimes improve if you stand by a window, though this isn't guaranteed. In desperation, seeking improvement outside on the balcony depends on the time of day and the weather. Mornings prove the most efficient while the afternoon will see you pulling your hair out in frustration, waving your phone about in the air and swearing at the device as the signal flips in and out. Exasperation often leads to leaving the mobile outside on the balcony railing, sneaking up to it after several minutes to see if the phone mast is awake and doing its stuff. Lulling you into a sense of false security, it'll be fine until you start talking and then it'll cut out resulting in one of those "Hello. Hello! HELLO!" conversations.

On a trip to the village for food supplies, we found Philippe standing outside his premises taking one of his frequent nicotine breaks and stopped for a chat. Lamenting the lack of a decent telephone signal, he raised our hopes by informing us cable was finally coming to the valley. The process of laying this piece of magic was to happen throughout the following summer. At last WiFi and instant connections would become a reality. We were ecstatic. It didn't last long, our euphoria short-lived as Phillippe hadn't quite finished delivering his news. *"Mais, c'est une rumeur."* We're still hoping the rumour has some basis in fact. Hope springs eternal so the saying goes.

Nailing Philippe down to any kind of lengthy conversation is hard during the summer months as his shop is always full, with a queue snaking outside. This almost merges with a similar queue at the *patisserie* next door, famous for selling a whole host of different types of fresh bread produced by the bakery across the road in the old town. The bread is joined by a collection of mouth-watering cakes and pastries, with early morning customers emptying the shelves of *pain au raisin*, *croissants* and *pain au chocolat* and leaving with armfuls of *baguettes*.

Philippe draws in the crowds with a mighty selection of organic, locally sourced meat, pates, *farcies*, huge slices of homemade quiches and a whole host of other delights, too many to mention here. In the summer months, helping things along is the aroma of free-range chickens, coated in Herbs de Provence, cooking on the rotisserie outside over a tray of potatoes, cut small, absorbing the juices. These never fail to make me and Rob drool, but there's only so much chicken the two of us can manage in one meal, so we tend to have a quarter each and use the rest in a curry, the sauce provided in a jar from a famous UK supermarket and transported by us for convenience. Trying to locate an Indian curry house in our surrounding mountains will be as fruitless as a search for a flock of dodos in New Zealand. As for the rest of Philippe's wares, there's not too much here to satisfy the vegetarian appetite, after all, it is a *boucherie*. Quiches filled with vegetables and free-range eggs give a nod to our non-meat eating friends, but if you're a vegan, forget it.

After getting over our disappointment regarding our commune's chances of becoming a fully-fledged member of the twenty-first century, we asked Philippe if he wanted to join us for a beer later. His happy response was a firm *"Oui, certainment!"* We arranged to meet at 7.00 pm at the tiny outside bar, ice cream parlour and occasional seafood seller, about four paces from his shop. This establishment is run by a couple of his chums we'd yet to meet properly and is only open during the holiday season. It consists of a baby bar table, surrounded by four stools. If these are occupied, people will sit on the public bench or the wall. We arrived at the appointed hour; the stools were vacant as most folk would be busy preparing dinner at home while supping and nibbling their way through apéritifs.

We settled ourselves in, ordering a beer while we waited for Philippe to emerge from his shop. He was rather late and our glasses were almost empty by the time he finally locked up and came over, greeting us in the way he always does with a cheery "Bobeeee! Jeanne!" His two friends, one of whom was the owner of this little place and another who appeared to be an assistant, shook hands as introductions were made. As always in situations like this, the minute Philippe told them we were *anglais* we were faced with conversations laced with unpredictable smatterings of English words and good-natured digs about Brexit.

About three glasses in, a roar announced the arrival of a motorbike. This proved to be a stunning machine possessing immaculate coachwork in bright red, including the mudguards, with pristine white-walled tyres beneath. Its gleaming chrome work sparkled in the evening sunshine and the leather seat appeared to have never suffered the weight of a human bottom! Rob informed me the make of the bike was an Indian. I thought it was a Harley Davidson, but what do I know?

Rob has owned a few motorbikes in the past and we often hired one in our younger days when enjoying a holiday abroad. After we'd become bored lying around on a beach or by a pool, a motorbike fulfilled our need to explore our environment, visiting interesting places before we wound up with sunburn and brain paralysis. He mourned the sale of his final bike and still hankers after another, but I remind him that at his age reactions are slowing, sight worsening and he's likely to wind up in hospital or worse. I think I'm being a caring wife. He thinks I'm a complete spoilsport.

The new arrival climbed from his bike and joined our merry gang. Discovering we were two Brits gate-crashing this small clique of happy, beer-sodden locals, he greeted us in perfect English. Turned out he'd picked it up working in the UK as a youth. There followed a couple of hours of conversation, jokes, jesting and jollity during which I asked nicely if I could take a photo of his beautiful bike. The nice owner graciously let me sit astride it, kindly using my phone camera to capture the moment, providing me with the opportunity to post the photo on Facebook and impress my friends. It 'sent' eventually, but if this had been a race between technology and carrier pigeon, the pigeon would have won.

15

Birthday

I t was my birthday. They come around far too quickly these days. As a youngster, I always believed people my age were not simply old, but positively decrepit with nothing to say that was the least bit relevant to my younger self. Oh, the arrogance of youth! I consider it a blessing to be waking up each morning and treat each birthday as an excuse to have a bloody good time! After all, attitude is a personal choice and age is just a number.

I greeted my day with a glance through the bedroom curtains. The sky was a spectacular shade of blue, undisturbed by clouds with the sun's rays picking out the fort which stood high on its vantage point down the valley, just visible from the window. The birds were tweeting and I could hear the ringing of cow bells as the herd meandered in haphazard procession up the field towards the forested slope to spend the day in the shade. It was going to be another hot one.

The aroma of coffee drifted up the stairs. Maisie had jumped on the bed earlier, impatient to be allowed out for a pee. Rob gave in to this canine persuasion after she enthusiastically bounded on his chest and began to clean his ears. After releasing the dogs to wander outside to relieve themselves, he'd prepped the coffee which was ready by the time I reached him in the kitchen. I grabbed my mobile to ensure the telephone mast was behaving as it should and was able to receive birthday calls from the 'kids' and the three grandchildren, making me wish they were here with us. I also picked up hordes of birthday messages on Facebook which never cease to make me feel truly humbled and lucky to have such lovely people in my life. Our son Ben, during his call, had informed me that a large parcel was on its way, but explained it appeared to be stuck in a depot somewhere in Paris and asked us to keep our eyes on the situation and check in regularly to find out what was going on.

Rob confirmed that lunch at one of our favourite restaurants further down the valley had been booked. He had also reserved our favourite table which sits beside a flower-filled trough topped with a little apex roof, beyond which lies a small lake filled with trout and beyond that, the ever-present mountains.

Arriving at the restaurant, we were welcomed with smiles from the lady owner who knows us well after our frequent visits throughout the years. We settled at our table, and the dogs flopped down in the shade next to us, keeping a beady eye out for any stray scraps that might come their way. Halfway through our delightful main course, the sun disappeared suddenly as a large black cloud emerged from behind the mountain ridge. Within minutes, the guests were grabbing meals, wine and cutlery and hurtling indoors as torrential rain lashed down accompanied by a gale-force wind which had come out of nowhere. The serving staff were rushing around retrieving flying place mats, chasing parasols and struggling to close others before they took flight. It was all over in a matter of minutes as the clouds rapidly moved away to drench more unsuspecting diners in the next valley. We remained indoors, along with all the other soggy guests, to finish our meals and wine while laughing about the vagaries of the weather in the mountains.

The Birthday Present

One of the beautiful things about being in the mountains, with little light pollution and crystal clear skies, is the amazing view of the heavens after dark. The night sky is saturated with stars. The Milky Way appears to hover just above the fingertips and the constellations are clearly visible. It's possible to track the space station as it moves through its path across the night sky, the moon shows off its surface and for those in the know, planets close to Earth can be pinpointed. We have always been fascinated and spent many a time, heads tilted backwards, gazing upwards, deliberating unknown answers to impossible questions about the universe.

My missing package from Ben finally dislodged itself from the Parisian storage depot having been proven not to be an explosive device and was finally delivered intact by a nice man in his yellow *La Poste* van. The box was large and heavy, covered with labels instructing me to 'open this way up' and 'handle with care'. My first thought was about the eye-watering cost of having it sent from the UK to our mountain bolthole, but my second thought was to get it open and see what lay in wait.

After noting the warning stickers and treating it like a baby, my present gradually materialized as Rob slowly retrieved it from its protective packaging. Ben had bought me the most beautiful telescope with which to explore the heavens.

Of course, I cried. Rob thinks I'm soppy. I admit I'm soppy. I can see nothing wrong with crying over a lovely present, Walt Disney's *Dumbo*, or a film with a sad ending, especially if a dog is involved. I rang Ben immediately, gushing thanks, heaping praise and telling him off for spending so much!

"It's not just yours though, Mum. Well it is, but I thought it might be a good idea to keep it at the house for us all to use when we're down there."

He's not wrong. It's a wonderful idea and I'm quite willing to share as long as everyone remembers who the owner is.

16

Three Wasp Tales

I n summer these stripy, stinging beasties are everywhere, building nests in places you really don't want to find them and setting up flight paths like a mini squadron flying back and forth to their base, usually directly in front of where you're sitting. When trying to enjoy lunch or dinner outside in the sunshine, they hover about trying to steal food from your plate and are extremely bad tempered if you try to bat one away.

Every year we face the possibility of finding a small wasps' nest or two, generally hidden behind a closed shutter, but these prove to be easily disposed of as their future inhabitants have only just commenced building work before it is fit for 'Her Royal Waspness' to take up residence. A quick spray usually sends them dashing for freedom or dying on the spot. However, we have good cause to be extremely careful as we think French wasps are particularly evil buggers. Here are three tales that prove it!

The first encounter, from what we believed to be a paper wasp, occurred a few years ago when Rob was stung. He had accidentally disturbed a couple of these vengeful creatures who were trying to take up residence behind the door of our external electricity box, accessing it by squeezing through a tiny gap. Rob was unable to move quickly enough before one launched at him, delivering the *coup de grace* straight into Rob's face, just below the eye. It was extremely painful. I gathered this when Rob starting shouting:

"Ow, ow, OW! One of those bloody wasps has just stung me. OW!"

I proceeded to peer at the targeted spot on his face, uttered soothing noises and told him it didn't look that bad. Suitable medications were applied to the sting and Rob was fussed over for the remainder of the evening. The offender and his friends had been dispatched shortly after the incident, the death spray worked almost instantaneously.

The following morning, Rob looked like something from a horror film. Pity this hadn't happened at Halloween as we'd have made a killing by hiring him out to scare children. Joking aside, it looked horrendous. The right side of his face had ballooned to a size I didn't think possible, his eye was swollen and tight shut and the skin was red. Many a time Rob has reacted to bites from mosquitos, flies or the odd sting, all resulting in minor swelling which disappeared after a few days, but I was concerned. This was a totally different ball game. Of course, Rob, being a 'bloke', decided he was going to tough it out, not wanting any fuss. He reassured me that he felt OK even it remained painful.

The reaction from Philippe when we visited his shop that morning was priceless. He took one look at Rob and was ready to call for an ambulance. We managed to placate him and agreed to visit the pharmacy instead. Our local pharmacy was closed, it being Sunday, so Philippe rushed into the Tourist Information to ask them if another was open somewhere nearby, then rushed back, confirming one in the next town further up the valley was open until lunchtime.

We headed off immediately. The *pharmacien* peered at Rob's face, asking him a range of questions before explaining her husband, a doctor, was arriving shortly and it might be wise for him to give Rob a quick once over. We hung around, sitting on the wall outside for a considerable time, but the mysterious doctor didn't appear, so his wife issued Rob with tablets and a special cream, adding that a visit to our local doctor would be advised.

The following morning, we found ourselves in the waiting room at the local clinic with Rob receiving some sympathetic stares from those already installed in the waiting room. As Brits, we are extremely well practised in queueing, whether on our feet or on our seated bottoms and know how to do it well, politely biding our time until it's our turn. We have acquired oodles of experience over the years in all kinds of situations, especially medical settings. Maybe it's a recognised skill that other nationalities believe we excel in and that is why we were totally ignored as numerous patients drifted in and out. We were just about to give up when a young GP finally called us through. He spoke English. Something we were pleased about as we're not particularly *au fait* speaking in French about *guêpes* (wasps) and their life cycles. As it was, we didn't need to identify the type of wasp, try to describe it, identify its gender or the components of its nest. In fact, we didn't have to say anything apart from confirming it was a wasp sting. After showing him the medication issued by the pharmacy, he agreed he would have prescribed the very same and that all should be well in around five days. He kindly didn't charge for his time either.

All predictions about the length of the recovery period were true with Rob's face returning to normal size and the pain slowly fading, but he has been incredibly cautious around wasps ever since.

The Paper Wasp's Revenge 2019

This happened in 2019 on a sunny warm morning not long after our arrival at Les Hirondelles. We needed to drag the outdoor dining furniture into the light by removing the rather tatty protective cover it had been hiding under since the previous summer.

I approached, intending to assist Rob when he rapidly backed away shouting:

"Wasps! Look, under the cover on the right corner where that tear is in the fabric. One has just flown out and it looks like the same type of wasp that stung me last time. I'm not going anywhere near those little ***tards."

I had to see for myself as I hadn't noticed any wasps and presumed it was a loner who was long gone. Yells from Rob telling me to back off didn't work as I bravely lifted the corner. Sure enough, several paper wasps (we think) were busy fashioning a nest, far too occupied to notice I'd just lifted off their roof.

Out came the death spray and while Rob watched from a distance, telling me to leave it and come away, I reassured him it would be fine. Gently lifting the corner and starting to spray, several of the blighters took to the air. I backed away to watch them all perish, but a couple blessed with a more robust constitution turned and flew after me. Resembling a scene from the OK Corral, I eventually stood firm with my trusty canister armed and ready, succeeding in shooting these vengeful creatures down in mid-air, but not before one of the sods stung me on my finger, right on the knuckle. Now I'm no baby when it comes to pain, after all, I've given birth twice, but admit this hurt.

"Ha! I did try to warn you, but as always, you didn't listen," said Rob.

Lotion was applied and I waited for the pain and swelling to disappear in a day or two. It didn't, taking days before I could bend my finger again without shouting "Ouch". Well, you live and learn.

The Common Wasp Mortuary Summer 2021

"Rob!" I shouted. "Come have a look at this!" I was standing in the small front bedroom staring at a minimum of twenty wasp corpses scattered on the floor under the window, with more under the bed.

Rob joined me as I explained in a worried voice that the room was spotless when we left the last time we were there. He was fairly calm, telling me they were probably flying about at the time we closed the house and then died because they couldn't get out. Within record time, a dustpan and brush ensured all evidence of mass starvation had been deposited in the bin.

The next morning after breakfast, I checked the room and all appeared well. I could stop worrying about further wasp invasions and concentrate on enjoying our holiday. How wrong I was. Over the next couple of weeks, the room became a mortuary for wasps. A couple were often detected in their final throes, soon to breathe their last after suffering the effects of the huge amounts of insecticide sprayed onto the wall, ceiling, floor and into every corner of the room. Entering almost killed me with the amount still lingering in the air. However, day after day, the wasps' remains kept appearing, sometimes numbering in the teens and sometimes in the tens. We knew there must be a nest, but simply couldn't locate it.

We headed off to the Hérault for our week's camping trip, knowing we'd face a pile of dead wasps when we returned, but there was little we could do, so we emptied another can of wasp destroyer, closed the door to the room and forgot about it until we arrived back.

The first thing I did when entering the house after our break was to head straight up to the wasp mortuary. The dead were exactly where we thought they'd be, scattered under the window mostly, but not the mountainous pile we expected to be wading through after a week away. It happily appeared the numbers were declining.

Once the bodies were disposed of, the room was sprayed copiously in every nook and cranny once more. After closing the door on the lethal concoction now wafting around the room, I was in desperate need of some fresh mountain air in order to dislodge the insecticide invading my nostrils. Sitting quietly outside doing nothing in particular except breathing fresh air, I spied several wasps heading in straight line formation towards the apex of the roof where the end of a wooden support beam jutted through the wall.

Rob was summoned and we both agreed we'd found the source of the nest. It was impossible for us to get anywhere near it. There was also no obvious entry into the house from under the roof either. Professional help was considered, but over the course of the next week, the number of bodies started to decrease rapidly to single figures. The spraying continued with Rob and me in danger of becoming bankrupt, spending a small fortune on the stuff, but the wasps were disappearing fast. Whether this was due to the spray or something Mother Nature had turned her hand to, we don't know. It could be that the queen had died of natural causes and joined her workers in wasp heaven or that the spray had finally penetrated the nest and the whole caboodle was as dead as a doornail.

By the end of our third week, we'd not seen hide nor hair, or more appropriately, 'wing or sting' of a wasp in the room for several days and were assured the things would not return after research revealed these annoying varmints refuse to inhabit an abandoned nest. Eventually, it dissolves into dust and is no more.

17

A Week of Heartbreak

Wasps now dealt with, we were entering our final week at the house and were determined to enjoy the time left before we had to clean up and depart for the UK. However, those sunny days we take for granted can be interrupted by darker times, helping to remind us that life is fleeting and to appreciate all we have. Little did we know what was awaiting us just around the corner as we planned our week ahead. It was the start of a journey which demonstrated just how transient life can be.

It was early morning. Rob and I were busy browsing our mobiles. We do this on a daily basis to ensure we don't miss any urgent emails, messages or posts from home or beyond. As I ploughed through, I opened a message informing the extended family that Rob's cousin had passed away with lung cancer aged seventy-two. It came as a bit of a shock as his family, abiding by his wishes, had kept his illness a secret from all but his wife, children and grandchildren. It had also happened very quickly with the diagnosis delivered only a few weeks before his death. As we were unable to do much from France, we sent a message of condolence to his wife and family and later confirmed we would be attending his funeral.

The following day my mobile rang. It was Ben explaining that our much-loved nephew had been taken to hospital. At this point, no one knew what was wrong, but Ben promised to ring us back when he had more news. No news is good news as the saying goes, so we didn't worry too much when Ben didn't come back to us over the next few days.

Two days later, an email lay in my inbox which delivered some very sad news. Our long-time French friends had lost their only child, Anthony, to a brain tumour. We were aware that he had this terminal condition, but it still hit us hard. We had met the family over thirty years earlier on one of our camping trips, had shared time with them at their home in the Vendee and they had spent time with us in the UK. We had attended Anthony's wedding in France and kept in regular touch with his parents, even having them stay at Les Hirondelles just three years previously. Anthony was only in his mid-forties, leaving behind his wife and his young teenage son and daughter.

The following day we finally received that call from Ben; tests revealed Andy had leukaemia. Ben and he were as close as brothers, being best friends since toddler days. Andy was Terry and Janice's son, so we had seen him grow from a baby into a loving husband and father. Ben was distraught, worrying about what might happen and presuming the worst-case scenario. All Rob and I could do was persuade him to stop thinking this and to await more news. It was incredibly hard being so far away. Rob managed to talk to a very worried Tez by phone, but there was little else we could do. We knew we had a difficult path to walk once we arrived home, but later learned Andy was to have immediate chemotherapy. The consultant was apparently very optimistic as the leukaemia had been discovered early and the prognosis was encouraging, predicting the likelihood of a full recovery.

All this bad news left us reeling, feeling very heavy-hearted, unable to shake ourselves out of it for a while. We realised we needed to pull ourselves together and that, in Andy's case, he had such a positive outlook that there remained a chink of brightness amidst the darkness; a light called hope.

Once back home in the UK and to do something useful, I got together with Andy's wife and members of his close family to run a ten-kilometre *Race for Life*, an organisation that raises funds for cancer charities. I'm not a runner and my hip hasn't been the same since, but I did it in memory of John and Anthony and in hope for Andy's return to full health, allowing him to continue living his life with his much-loved wife and two young sons.

Later that year, hope and optimism faded as Andy devastatingly and unexpectedly passed away on 18th November 2021 aged forty-three.

PART III

AUTUMN STORIES

18

Doggie Travel Documents ... and Ferrets!

Chatting to the lovely Liverpudlian lady who was dealing with my Tunnel booking, I was bemoaning the cost of the Pet Health Certificate. She heartily agreed, explaining many customers she'd dealt with were fuming about the situation. I felt slightly better when she informed me one lady, wishing to take her dog to France, had been forced by her vet to pay £400 for the certificate. I presumed her vet was situated somewhere posh, like Knightsbridge or Chelsea in London, where he felt compelled to fleece the wealthy. Between the sympathetic noises and tales of woe, the booking lady provided a nugget of information that would eventually release us from the shackles of this complicated and expensive nonsense.

It appeared one of her customers had secured, quite legally, an EU French Pet Passport for their dog. Just what it entailed remained a mystery, but I was determined to find out in time for travel this October. Research revealed recent legislation from the French Government stated it was now permissible for holiday homeowners to acquire a Pet Passport for their dog, cat or ferret.

I have to admit, I've often puzzled about the inclusion of a ferret. Do people take their pet ferrets to France? Is there a ferret society that lobbied the government when Pet Passports were introduced? Maybe these furry, trouser leg escapologists are an extremely popular critter in France. Who knows?

In case any of you are mystified by the trouser leg reference, let me explain. There's a bizarre endurance competition called ferret-legging, involving stuffing several ferrets into the trousers of the obviously unhinged participants in order to test their manhood. I doubt any manhood is left after the ferrets' sharp teeth and claws have had a field day, fighting to escape from their belted and ankle-tied prison. Apparently this 'sport' was popular amongst Yorkshire miners in the '70s, no doubt to prevent boredom on the picket lines during the miners' strikes at the time. It isn't quite so popular these days. I wonder why?

Placing the subject of ferrets to one side, there were rules to be followed before a Pet Passport could be considered. As we still needed to get to France, we had to secure a certificate first. We headed back to the vet who had issued the original document the previous summer, and were told prices had risen (surprise, surprise), but after some assertiveness from us about why this was outrageous followed by some pleading to push the receptionist and the head of the practice towards a satisfactory outcome, we finally secured a certificate for a bargain price. As they had a duplicate online, the only requirements were to change the dates, serial number and stamp it.

19

Teddy's Toe and a Conundrum

O ur day of departure was approaching. Teddy was now devoid of a toe, having had it removed after a lump appeared which drove him demented. I was worried he'd chew the thing off himself, but the vet removed it instead. The lump was checked at the lab and proved to be harmless and the doggie insurance paid the humongous fee without any argument. Teddy adopted his 'poor me' look for a couple of days, but couldn't maintain it as the great outdoors beckoned with the promise of a romp around a grassy field with a ball.

I too had to face medical intervention. We were now in that 'post-Covid' situation where doctors appeared to have adopted their lockdown lifestyles and only saw patients after discussing it first by telephone. I still wonder how they can diagnose many conditions accurately without the need to actually examine a patient. It took three thirty-five minute phone calls to get through to the surgery, a two-week wait for the telephone appointment, to be told by a receptionist it was basically my fault for choosing the most popular doctor in the surgery! After a month I finally saw the doctor face to face, only to suffer the indignity of being informed I was showing mild signs of osteoarthritis in one joint because of a lifelong love of participating in sport and fitness. I say indignity, as this news was accompanied by "Well, you have to expect this kind of thing at your age." Thanks doc.

I often wonder about this. Here's the conundrum. We hear, over and over about the advantages of keeping ourselves fit and healthy. We grab our footballs and netballs, we pound the roads in expensive running trainers, we cycle for miles, we hike, play tennis or maybe spend a fortune on a gym membership, being tortured as we lift heavy weights or reach exhaustion on the rowing machine. Whatever we choose to do, we're told to keep it up as it's good for us and keeps the horrors of old age at bay. So we continue until we're told to stop because joints are heading towards the totally knackered stage and we'll be waiting for years to have bits replaced. Added to this, we're told as we age, our metabolism slows, so now it's time to cut back on the amount we eat in case we begin to gain too much weight, which we probably will as we're taking things a lot more easily or doing nothing at all because our replacement joint operation hasn't happened yet. Fat and unfit, the old ticker begins to suffer, climbing stairs becomes impossible without the aid of an oxygen mask and eventually we keel over and die because, guess what, we didn't keep ourselves fit!

I reassured the doctor I would not be persuaded to give up my much-loved fitness classes, my skiing or anything else for that matter. She did agree about the sporty stuff, but recommended I not leap around quite so enthusiastically in my classes from now on. I took her advice, leaping around a little less than before, have taken up Pilates as it's good for joints and am 'filling my boots' daily with a load of joint-recommended supplements. There was some good news as she explained my heart rate, blood pressure and cholesterol were astonishing … for a woman of my age! I am not in my dotage!!! Ever felt like giving your doctor a slap? Figuratively speaking of course.

20

The Limousine

A few days before we left for France, we were out with some of Rob's old apprentice mates. Meeting at sixteen years old, they shared many happy days when they possessed little common sense, raging hormones and a tendency towards committing outrageous practical jokes on one another, usually in the apprentice training school; perfect fodder for reminiscing now they're older with less hair and a few ailments.

One is a real petrolhead and due to having started a successful business which flourished through his sheer hard work, has been rewarded with a comfortable retirement, spending time restoring old vehicles. He is also in a position to buy brand-new ones whenever he likes, swapping them nearly as often as he changes his underpants. This particular evening he arrived in a new, top-of-the-range Landrover Defender which he later told us he wasn't keen on due to it not driving as well as the old models. He's a proper traditionalist when it comes to driving.

"How would you like to take it to France? It could do with a long journey to see how it performs. Just leave your old Discovery with me and you can borrow it if you like."

Rob asked me if we ought to take up the offer. The fact this new limousine was unlikely to have major bits drop off it, my reply was definitely in the affirmative. If it had been mine, I wouldn't have let it out of my sight. I would be driving about showing off and warning the dogs every time they attempted to put a paw outside of their allotted seating area. Our friend, on the other hand, was perfectly happy to allow us to drive it hundreds of miles through France, even knowing our history of mishaps when it comes to motor vehicles. Now that's what I call friendship!

Two days later, we were heading for the Tunnel in our fabulous new vehicle, leaving our old Discovery behind for our friend to enjoy.

While we were still in France, our friend sold the Defender back to the garage he'd bought it from a few months before. They'd been in contact several times asking him if would be willing to return it and make a hefty profit in the process. He explained it was currently in France with friends, but the garage had customers queuing up to buy and were willing to wait until our return. These vehicles were as rare as hen's teeth and deliveries were taking forever, so the garage had willing victims on hold to pay an eye-watering amount to get their hands on one. Our friend happily took his profit and bought another car, a Landrover Discovery that was older than ours! "He's so jammy, he'd fall off the top of Rackhams[1] into a new suit!" I said to Rob.

Overnighters

Our first night was spent in a small, modest hotel we always use in the delightful Flemish market town of St Omer, a key staging post between London and Paris many centuries ago. It's a place we've yet to explore thoroughly, never finding the time in our overnight stays to check out the network of canals in the lower town or the Marais Audomarois, a UNESCO-listed biosphere reserve. What we have managed, is to wander through the narrow streets which span out from the cobbled grand square. In summer, numerous restaurants spill onto the surrounding pathways, creating a lively and happy atmosphere, watched over by a magnificent 200 year-old Italianate theatre building. We have promised ourselves a longer visit in the near future.

The good weather stayed with us as we travelled south towards our second night's accommodation near Lyon, arriving hungry and tired. Their dining room wasn't open, but a friendly young receptionist directed us to a large buffet restaurant across the street. Dogs were forbidden to enter, forcing me to linger at the door while Rob meandered around counters laden with a huge variety of food, filling one of those sectioned polystyrene boxes with his choices. He also managed to persuade the staff to sell him a bottle of wine, which they kindly opened, the cork replaced loosely to allow for transportation. As Rob took his turn to hang around by the door, I shoved what I could into my box. It was one of those occasions when you're so overwhelmed by the choices, you leave with a collection of totally unrelated items normally not seen together on the same plate.

We headed back to the hotel and settled at a dining room table in near darkness. Our choice of table enabled us to take full advantage of the light straying in from the reception area, aided by the gentle glow provided by a couple of lampposts outside the window, together forming the only other illumination. Thankfully, the receptionist took pity on us and fetched cutlery and glasses from the abandoned kitchen, saving us the embarrassment of having to eat with our fingers and glug wine directly from the bottle, though why she decided to refrain from turning on the main lights remained a mystery.

The main aim on this break at the house was to re-varnish the shutters as they were looking decidedly shabby, but they would have to wait until the usual forest of weeds was pulled up and shouted at for re-seeding themselves. Gilbert was in residence, minus Annie, as he'd been spending time painting his own shutters, a job he disliked intensely he told us, wrinkling his nose at the thought. He was heading back home the following day and would return with Annie a couple of days after that. He was excited as he had a new Fiat Panda on order and couldn't wait to collect it.

Our little commune was quiet, as summer visitors were long gone and the family who had bought Gabriel and Marcella's house below us on the road, had also stopped their banging and drilling as they'd returned back from whence they came, for now at least. We're hoping they'll finish the restoration of the interior soon and start on the exterior, especially the rusty metal roof and the chimney which is held together with tape and clogged with what looks like lumps of black, sooty tar. I only hope they don't risk lighting a fire!

October days are short, generally with warm sunshine, but temperatures plunge once the sun starts to slip behind the mountains, prompting us to gather the logs for the fire from the store underneath the balcony. Surrounded by pine trees, a collection of cones is gathered and kept dry to be used as kindling. Within minutes the fire is roaring away, the house snug and toasty. We then curl up on the sofas reading a book with soft music playing in the background, or maybe choose to watch a favourite TV programme or film while enjoying a glass of wine to wash down dinner. The dogs are sleeping, stretched out on the rug or more often, taking up room beside us both on the sofas. They refuse to share, so Teddy settles next to Rob on one and Maisie next to me on the other.

Early morning and a view through the window will reveal a frosty covering in the fields below our commune and a sparkling, slippery coating adorning the balcony. It's cold enough to turn breath into vapour, forcing us to reach for something woolly and warm; a reminder that winter is waiting in the wings. For now, once the sun's rays pierce the shadows, the frost disappears and the air starts to warm considerably. We are always amazed at just how warm it does get, forcing us to discard our cold weather woollies and don a tee shirt.

---

1. (Explanations for non-Brummies – 'jammy' means someone who is frequently lucky or fortunate and 'Rackhams' is a Harrods-type store in the city centre.)

21

Sheep and their Deposits

I t was time for the annual *Transhumance* when hundreds of sheep would be brought from their mountain pastures before winter sets in. Routes down are often blocked by these vast woolly oceans, with shepherds (*bergers* in French) and their dogs working hard to push the sheep to one side, allowing enough room for a motorist to slowly negotiate their way past. Notices around the town advertised the festival to celebrate the event. We hadn't been for a few years, missing out as it was held at a time when we were absent. Thankfully, the celebration coincided with our visit and we were excited to see this extravaganza of sheep and shepherds once more. We arrived before the procession was due to start in order to gain a good position. A small group of musicians, dressed in antiquated clothing, were playing a series of tunes, some of which were definitely not medieval as I recognised a few of our UK chart toppers and was tempted to burst into song and dance around the car park. Rob would have been mortified, so I restricted my enthusiasm to modest foot-tapping and singing quietly to myself.

The sheep failed to be impressed by the musical accompaniment and took no notice. The flock's full attention carried on eating as they continued their absent-minded grazing, dotted about the field next to where we were standing. High above, the Fort de Savoie loomed on its rocky outcrop, set against a deep blue sky surrounded by a full pallet of autumn colour. A walk up to it was planned for later. The views across the walled medieval town were ripe for photography; the perfect image as it nestled in the valley alongside the river Verdon, the surrounding mountains clothed in vibrant seasonal foliage.

Getting slightly chilly waiting around, we finally became aware that the procession was imminent and looked towards the field where an invisible signal brought the patous dogs to attention. The sheep reluctantly stopped their munching and were herded out of the field onto the road to begin their slow amble towards the walls of the old town. The musicians led the cavalcade of sheep, shepherds, dogs, bystanders and a donkey slowly towards the Porte de Savoie, the entrance to the old town. The shepherds knowingly positioned themselves within the flock so any escapees could be quickly brought back into line. Rob and I, along with many others, stayed with the sheep as they were guided through the narrow streets, but eventually ran ahead to secure a good spot outside the church. Mind you, it didn't feel that good when a large woolly specimen trod on my foot leaving behind a lovely hoof print consisting of faecal matter. I wasn't best pleased as my boots were new and beige in colour. I'd also spoken nicely to the creature just before it nearly broke my toe and left its calling card. We hung on long enough to witness the blessing of the sheep by the local priest before heading towards a freshwater fountain to commence the cleaning process, carefully stepping around the enormous amount of sheep poo that now lined the streets. Happily, I succeeded in removing the worst of it, but the sheep's faded signature still remains to this day.

Shutters and Daniel's Tale

The weather continued in a string of sunny days and cold nights and life continued with visits to the town for food stuffs. Philippe was on holiday, visiting family in the Carmargue, leaving his sons in charge of the shop and Gilbert had arrived back with Annie, who was spending time tidying up her small flower plots, shrubs and tubs. With our green-fingered jobs out of the way, we'd managed to spend days walking in the mountains, with the dogs bounding along beside us, following routes we've come to know well. We have always loved our time spent strolling through such wonderful scenery, marvelling at every turn, and feeling privileged to have discovered our little property in such a beautiful part of the world.

Enjoying a lazy afternoon, reading from my Kindle on the balcony in the sunshine, I realised it was time we tackled the shutters. Gilbert's were immaculate and ours were peeling, cracked and looking unloved. The first task was to purchase the varnish. Now anyone who read my first book will know that our local DIY sells paint and associated products at eye-watering prices, so we decided to head off for a forty-minute drive to the large DIY store in Dignes les Bains instead. As always happens, you go to buy something specific and wind up buying more than intended.

"You know we planned to change the ancient radiators?" I said, "I've found some new ones and they're a real bargain!"

A short while later with the credit card having been abused a little more than intended, we left the store with our tin of varnish and three of the 'real bargains'!

A plan was hatched. Rob would install the new radiators while I tackled the shutters. Rob was capable of doing both jobs, but the extent of my electrical knowledge stops at changing a light bulb or replacing a fuse in a plug, so my skilled hubby, who is completely *au fait* with high-powered wires and currents, was the natural and only choice to mess with the bizarre French wiring.

The supports onto which I would lay each shutter door were kept in the sous-sol, so it was Rob's job to retrieve these. As you all know, I don't venture into the spider hole unless I have the possibility of dressing in a full Tyvek body suit with the hood pulled up (the suits worn by forensic teams at a murder scene), which is not something you have just lying casually in your wardrobe. I also needed help lifting the shutters from their hinges.

I really don't mind painting or varnishing as it can be quite therapeutic, but I loathe the preparation and these shutters were in need of a hefty sanding before a brush went anywhere near them. We borrowed Gilbert's sander and I set up work in a sunny spot on the grass just below the balcony. The sun was hot and the drying process was short, meaning the many coats needed would take half the time.

Absorbed as I sloshed varnish everywhere, I didn't hear our farmer neighbour, Daniel, approaching until he was standing at my shoulder, making me jump and almost drowning him in 'medium oak'. We hadn't seen him for a while, but he was, as usual, full of *joie de vivre*. Hearing his voice, Rob joined us, shortly followed by Gilbert. The banter went on for quite a while, with our farmer admiring the fact I was working *tres dur*, very hard, while Rob appeared to be doing *rien*, nothing. I, of course, joined in the joshing, with Rob as the target. It was all very jovial and it felt great to be standing in the sunshine laughing with our lovely neighbours like old friends.

Daniel's Provençal French, spoken at speed, has always been difficult to understand, but he appeared to slow things down for us on this occasion, so we grasped most of what he was saying. Once Rob's turn in the ribbing spotlight had passed, Daniel enquired if we knew a certain gentleman who lived in the valley. After providing us with a description, we pondered for a while as to who it might be. Further clues and a bit of a Q&A session finally turned on the light bulb and we were able to acknowledge we sometimes stopped for a quick chat if we spotted him out and about. Daniel was pleased we knew the man as it would lend more kudos to the story he was about to regale us with. It concerned the gentleman's wife who had sadly died a couple of years previously. We remembered seeing her before her demise, but never became acquainted, vaguely recalling she wasn't in the best of health with her age difficult to define.

Now losing someone is awful and we're testament to the suffering it causes, but Daniel was delighting in telling us this remarkable tale which described the means of her demise. According to our storyteller, she had a soft spot for alcohol and cigarettes, with her health failing for years because of this. It seems she did nothing to improve her lifestyle, eventually winding up in the local hospital. She suffered from extreme breathing difficulties and was therefore dependent on oxygen supplied by the cylinder next to her. Refusing to cease smoking, she apparently made the mistake of lighting up with the oxygen still running from the cylinder.

"Boom!!!" said Daniel, throwing his arms in the air, making me jump, before adding a second "boom" for effect. "Who lights a match next to an oxygen cylinder?" He was astonished anyone would be so *stupide*.

It seems the poor lady succeeded in blowing herself up and was the cause of a major fire in the hospital. Knowing how the local grapevine works in the valley, we think Daniel became somewhat carried away and stretched the truth a little. To complete his tale, his voice took on a dramatic tone,

"L'hôpital a brûlé! C'était une catastrophe!"

The whole hospital had burned to the ground, he explained, his expression displaying a look of utter disbelief.

It was a dreadful and tragic end to a life. We unanimously agreed it was a terrible way to go, but wickedly, the way Daniel recounted this awful event displaying enormous enthusiasm, and adding sound effects to his manic gesticulations, made us giggle. Not at the tragedy I hasten to add, but at Daniel and his storytelling antics.

We did bump into the widower later and he told us that the locals had been wonderful, full of sympathy, kindly supporting him and turning out in droves for his wife's funeral. I've no doubt that Daniel was someone who would have been counted among their numbers.

22

Olivier the Salesman

We met Olivier not long after moving into Les Hirondelles. He's a lovely guy who has made good from the humble beginnings in which we found him, his wife and son so many years ago, living in a tiny one-roomed house in our commune. His determination and hard work have resulted in a fairly successful *Electro-Menage* business in the village and we were thrilled when we discovered this. It continues to thrive and his shop caters to those needing new household appliances and a range of technical and electrical equipment. He was born in the UK but has lost much of his English after living in France for most of his life. One of the things he hasn't lost is his ability to talk non-stop.

One day Rob had the chance to call into his shop. I was still on varnishing duty when Rob appeared:

"I need to go out." He announced.

"Where?" I replied. "Thought you were installing the new radiators?"

"I am, but I need a special fuse and I thought I'd give Olivier's electrical shop a go. I know they don't stock them in the DIY."

He headed off while I happily continued with the final coats. The amount of time needed to drive down, buy a fuse and return should have been relatively short, but the clock informed me he'd been gone for nearly an hour. I was wondering where he'd got to. Just as I was thinking he'd broken down or worse, I heard the car approach along the track and park up. Rob was soon standing in front of me, sporting a grin.

"Where on earth have you been? How long does it take to buy a fuse? Couldn't Olivier find one?"

"Sorry. Not my fault. I bought the fuse. In fact, Olivier found it pretty quickly. I was ready to pay for it and leave but he was his usual non-stop chatty self. Not just that, I couldn't get away because he asked me to wait while he disappeared into the back office. He came out waving a brochure and tried to sell me a bed!"

"What? A bed? But he sells electrical stuff and appliances."

"You know what he's like. He'd sell sand to the Arabs. Turned out it was a sales brochure and I could see he was determined to plough through every make and model featured, especially the king-sized ones. I tried to tell him I only wanted the fuse, but as always he just carried on showing me photos of beds and saying he'd do a good deal on the price."

"So how did you make your escape then?"

"I just told him that he'd be our first choice if we ever needed a new bed. He seemed quite happy with that. Sold me the fuse, shook my hand and I made my escape before he found something else he wanted to flog me."

"Typical Olivier. Can't help but admire his persistence, bless him. Nothing changes."

23

Entertainment at the Vets

It was that time again when we needed to visit the local vet in a town further down the valley. Teddy and Maisie were in need of the required medication and completion of their Pet Health Certificate. However, on this occasion, we were also seeking to acquire the EU French Pet Passport, fulfilling the legal requirements by having a permanent address in France and adding to the government coffers by paying all our resident taxes on time.

A couple of days previously, we'd asked Gilbert if he would telephone the vet's receptionist to check if they actually had them in stock, would agree to supply them and make an appointment. The answer was affirmative, with no appointment necessary. We could pop in any time.

The lack of needing an appointment has generally been the case, but the downside is often the length of time you have to wait once you arrive. There may only be one other person in the waiting room, but the locals seem determined to utilise as much time as possible once allowed into the inner sanctum, regardless of what might be the circumstances regarding their sick animal. Those waiting are subjected to hearing loud conversations, often jovial, which last for an interminably long time. This merriment continues as the door opens revealing our gregarious vet who, dressed as usual in his black, woollen beanie hat, enjoys a load of cheery banter as he says *au revoir* to his clients. We've learned he is a past master at teasing and joke telling and possesses a particular talent for charming the ladies.

Over the years, although he replaced our old vet after his death, he hasn't changed a thing with regards to the décor inside the premises. The *cabinet* remains in the tiny detached single-storey building and the waiting area still boasts the half-dozen, ageing mismatched chairs. The old, wooden reception desk shows no improvement, its surface still displaying the bell, telephone and assorted paperwork, with often a large pile of cardboard boxes stacked on the floor behind, probably a recent delivery of veterinary medicines soon to be casually placed on the shelving above. The examination room is also unchanged, apart from a few new posters on the wall.

What hasn't changed is the fact that, like the vet before him, our replacement vet plucks random fees out of mid-air when the time arrives to pay the bill. When needing the official documentation for the dogs' return to the UK, we have yet to pay the same amount twice as he changes it from one visit to the next, sometimes lower, sometimes higher, probably depending on his mood or what he thinks he can get away with. Over time we've become used to the casual appearance of the premises and also more at ease with some of the slightly unusual animal care practices we've witnessed, but what we observed on this visit, really made us sit up and take notice.

We arrived at 11.00 am. Our vet only works half days at the surgery, closing up at 12.30 pm. A long-haired white dog, at least the size and stature of a St Bernard, was happily snoozing on the tiled floor. His lady owner was sitting patiently, hand clasped to the dog's lead. One other person was chatting to the vet inside his treatment room. We smiled at the receptionist/nurse/helper, hereon in called the 'assistant', who smiled, ignored us and disappeared to join the vet. Eventually, a female client and her pet cat emerged from the examination room, her face beaming as she offered her thanks to our vet. Maybe this reaction was due to his heroism in saving the moggie's life, or possibly she was just glowing, having been subjected to his full charm offensive!

After the cat and its happy owner said her *au revoirs* and left, the vet turned his attention to the lady with the white dog, explaining something to her and briefly nodding towards us in recognition before disappearing once again behind his door. Time ticked on and it was now well past 11.30 am. before he finally emerged carrying a syringe, the contents of which he administered to the dog lying prostrate at the owner's feet. The lady owner seemed perfectly at ease with this, while we watched on in shock as the dog drifted into a heavy anaesthetised sleep, his tongue lolling towards the floor.

"Blimey," whispered Rob, "he'd never get away with that at home. Surely he's not going to operate out here."

"Can't see how he's going to get that huge dog into his room and onto the examination table," I whispered back. "It'll weigh a ton! Besides, isn't it normal to weigh the dog before it's anaesthetised to make sure it doesn't wake up mid-procedure or doesn't wake up at all?"

The vet appeared after ten minutes and checked the dog was well and truly knocked out before the next stage of the process. Rob and I watched on in wide-eyed amazement as he rolled the dog onto its back and held onto one of the front legs. The owner grabbed the other, while the assistant had the job of clinging onto the hind legs. The dog hung limply, tongue still flopping from its mouth as it was lifted just clear of the floor. All three then shuffled slowly towards the examination room, looking rather red-faced with the effort. The door was kicked shut. We both turned and stared at one another in total disbelief.

A couple of minutes later the owner reappeared and sat down to wait, appearing not the least concerned at what had just happened. Not long afterwards, the vet called her into the examination room and the three of them repeated the process in reverse. Once the dog was back on the floor in its original spot, we could see evidence of a minor procedure. The hair had been shaved from a small area on the dog's flank and the staining of yellow antibacterial agent was evident around the bandaging. The poor dog was still flat out. A good job too, as the woman's husband arrived shortly afterwards and together they carried their dog in the same undignified manner to their car, laid it on the floor as the car door was opened, then, with some difficulty, heaved it onto the back seat.

"Crikey." I said. "Poor dog will be full of bruises after its owners dumped it on the floor like a sack of potatoes. Looked a bit brutal. Besides, shouldn't the dog be monitored until it comes around? What is it with these country vets?"

"Dunno," said Rob. "Bit of a strange way to go about things. I suppose it's just the way they do things around here. Remember how the old vet trussed up Max all those years ago, lashing his legs together with rope? That turned out OK. Think they're just used to dealing with farm animals and sheep wandering around the mountains, so I'm sure the vet knows what he's doing. Bit unconventional though."

The time had flown by as the unplanned entertainment had kept us transfixed. At last, our happy vet ushered us into the examination room, completed the necessary details on the Pet Health Certificate and gave us the tiny tablets for the dogs. We reminded him about the Pet Passports.

"Ah, you want *les passeportes,*" he said while grabbing two blank ones from a shelf. "You take. You fill in and bring back. I sign and *voila,* it's done."

He was obviously in a hurry to go to his very late lunch and didn't want to be bothered copying out the information from our old UK Pet Passports into the new ones. He then pulled a random figure out of the air for his fee and once we'd greased his palm with the required amount of cash, he stated with a smile, as he often does, "I just a poor vet," while tucking the money into his pocket.

"Hiding from the taxman again," said Rob knowingly as we wandered back outside.

"Poor vet indeed! Having said that, I don't care one jot if he's got a trunk full of non-declared booty under his bed! His fees are still less than half of those charged by our UK vets!"

The following morning, I neatly and very carefully copied our dogs' details into the new passports, leaving the security pages and the ones requiring proof of rabies vaccination blank for the vet to deal with. The next day we were back in the waiting room. On this occasion, no entertainment was forthcoming to provide a distraction as we patiently waited while our vet enjoyed the lengthy gossip and conversation provided by his clients. We were, as usual, the last in the waiting room, but it didn't take long for the vet to complete the necessary details and hand them back with a flourish.

"Your dogs have *passeport*! The douane will be happy, you will be happy, you go back to England and come back to France easy now."

I gleefully showed the dogs their new passports and announced they were now officially French. They remained unimpressed.

24

Chateauneuf en Auxios

Lindy is a smashing English lady who shares her time between an apartment in Paris and a pretty house in Burgundy. She and her French husband are working hard to lovingly restore it. I'd never met Lindy, but got to know her through an author website we're both members of and later through a long text chat on WhatsApp. This was conducted while Rob and I were on our way to Les Hirondelles and she was currently alone in her countryside home trying to deal with some serious leaks caused by very heavy rainfall. We chatted for quite a while and Lindy suggested it would be lovely to meet in person if we could somehow arrange to pop in and see her on our homeward journey.

Before leaving to return back to the UK, I booked a hotel in the hilltop village of Chateauneuf en Auxois. As we approached the area, we could see the *chateau*, a commanding presence towering above the surrounding countryside. We continued up a steep and winding road, finally entering the village and spending at least twenty minutes driving up and down the tiny streets trying to locate our hotel. I wouldn't mind, but the village is really small and we must have driven past our lodging several times without noticing it. Blink and you'd miss it. Finding ourselves on the route out of the village, we were forced to turn the Defender around on a road no wider than the width of a horse's cart. This involved some delicate manoeuvring to avoid removing paint from the car by scraping the walls of a couple of houses. In the end, we decided to locate our lodging on foot. Leaving the dogs in charge of the vehicle, with instructions to growl menacingly should a car thief attempt entry, we sauntered up a short steep incline to find the premises right next to the *chateau's* entrance. We were deliriously happy to have found it. The weather was grey and damp and darkness was rapidly approaching, exaggerating the chill in the air. The tiny hotel windows were bleeding light into the gloom, hinting at warmth and welcome, beckoning us in with the promise of a good meal and a comfy bed.

After finding the one and only parking spot outside the hotel, we grabbed the dogs and headed indoors. We were immediately transported back in time. The walls were old stone, with beams aplenty above our heads and a log fire roaring away in a huge raised hearth fitted with an iron rotisserie and turning handle. It was big enough to roast a whole sheep. Not only was the fire warm, but also the welcome we received from the owner, who, after the checking-in process had been conducted, presented us with a large key to our tiny room accessed by a climb up a narrow wooden staircase. It was one of those places where history comes alive, sleeping between walls that had been constructed in the fourteenth century or maybe earlier as the chateau itself was built in the tenth century. Thankfully, modernity was present in the shape of a radiator and a lovely shower room. After a wonderful meal in the small restaurant we returned to our cosy room and it wasn't long before Rob was doing his impression of a warthog and I finally drifted off with the aid of two earplugs. The dogs were settled on their beds and all was quiet. The following morning we awoke to the sound of pouring rain lashing the window and a small dog comfortably curled between us on the bed, twitching in her sleep!

We knew Lindy was going to provide a late breakfast, so refused the offer of one at the hotel, but gladly accepted a nice warming cup of milky coffee, slowly sipping it while watching the rain pelting down outside. Knowing we only had a short time to explore this unique and amazing little village before leaving, we reluctantly left the cocoon of the snuggly hotel reception and braved the torrential rain. We would have loved to enter the *chateau*, but it was closed on Sundays. It would have to wait until we ventured here again. With what little time we had to spare, we pulled out the golf brollies and strolled through the tiny street, amazed at the tall narrow buildings and a tiny square housing the mairie (Town Hall). The buildings were constructed using the same ancient stone as the little hotel, with wooden doorways directly off the street. It was a charming little place, and we could see why it had been accepted as one of the *Plus Beau Villages en France*, but we had to halt our wanderings and head back to the car before too much time had slipped away. We didn't want to be late for our rendezvous.

We found Lindy's lovely old property without getting lost and were welcomed warmly. It was great meeting her face to face, sharing a late breakfast and being given a guided tour of the house and grounds and explanations about what work had been done and the enormous amount still left to do. We agreed it's going to be a stunning home. With time ticking and a long journey for us to reach our final night's hotel in Calais, we had to leave and say our goodbyes, promising we'd return to check on progress and share more time together.

This might be sooner rather than later as I managed to leave my precious Wimbledon Tennis brolly behind. I know what you're thinking. What's so precious about an umbrella? Well, it's because attending the tournament had been on my bucket list since a young teen and took years and years to realise. Obtaining a ticket is difficult unless you're a celebrity, a member of the club or wealthy. For us normal folk it meant camping out, queueing for hours or applying for the ballot. A tennis mad friend and I had applied multiple times, each year resulting in disappointment, but finally it happened and we were allocated seats on No. 1 court before it had a roof. That brolly is a symbol of a dream realised, even if we only witnessed twenty minutes of play due to rain causing all matches to be called off. Hence the brolly's purchase. At least we got our money back on the tickets!

25

Dog Passport Trouble

Teddy and Maisie's French citizenship lasted a total of three days, as standing in front of a pleasant young lady in the Pet Reception at the tunnel, she explained the passports contained a couple of errors. A supervisor was summoned. Error one was on Maisie's passport. Our vet had inexplicably written the date of the chip insertion and not the date of birth on the page covered by the cellophane seal. Error two occurred on both passports. The supervisor stated they wanted the brand name of the rabies vaccination given and its serial number. I fished out our original UK pet passports to show her these details, but it wasn't going to wash. Officialdom won and our dog's newly acquired citizenship was revoked. I flourished the multi-paged Health Certificate instead. No longer *chiens*, the document confirmed their UK healthy dog status and they were permitted to leave these foreign shores. Finally, on home turf, we commenced our journey back to the Midlands, immediately fighting our way through a network of traffic-clogged UK motorways. With plenty of time between the stops and starts, we had ample opportunity to discuss what our next move could be in this whole dog travel debacle.

Not being hedge fund managers or CEOs of major corporations, we needed to avoid the huge expense and worry of going through the Pet Health Certificate rigmarole again. The Pet Passports required simple amendments in time for our next trip. I had a plan but we'd need to call upon Gilbert once again for his help.

Off went the email asking if he was due to visit his little house within the next few weeks and if so, would he mind popping into the vet's for us. His email arrived the following day saying he was happy to help.

In order to ensure there were no mistakes this time, I took and downloaded photos of the three pages requiring corrections or additions and printed these out, carefully circling the errors to make things obviously clear. The packet containing these, plus the UK and French passports, were duly posted to Gilbert with the hope our French vet would understand my scribbles.

Two weeks later the postman delivered a nice padded envelope, sent by Gilbert, which contained the old passports and two completely new ones. Of course, these attracted additional payment, but after I'd microscopically checked each and found nothing amiss, I couldn't have cared less. Finally, with stress levels returning to normal, concerns about obtaining Pet Health Certificates in future could be cast onto the rubbish heap of forgotten problems.

PART IV

WINTERTIME SAGAS

26

Maisie's Operation and Updating the Tech

We were looking forward to being back on the snow after missing out due to Covid the previous February, but this awful plague still had teeth and was re-emerging to cause chaos once more. With the new variant spreading throughout the population like wildfire, the government instituted new measures from 30th November 2021, hoping to hold back further spread. Masks would become compulsory in shops and on public transport again, with a day two PCR test required for those returning from abroad. We monitored the situation closely, hoping that, as was the current thinking, the Omicron variant wasn't the deadly killer its predecessor proved to be and that further restrictions wouldn't happen.

During 2021, like anyone wishing to travel abroad, we'd jumped through every hoop; having vaccinations, taking the expensive tests for outward and return journeys and completing health declarations and locator forms. We now kept our fingers tightly crossed as we headed towards the festive season and into the New Year, hoping these things would not reappear any time soon or that we'd be forced to cancel our winter break in February.

Thankfully, all turned out well with the French government decreeing that from 14th February, no testing or other restrictions would be necessary for those wishing to travel from the UK, with testing for return into the UK had also being lifted. Only proof of vaccination was needed. We were over the moon. Life could return to normal.

It was two days before Christmas. That particular morning, I'd woken to find our little dog Maisie looking ill and in pain, her eye half closed and weeping. There was obviously something seriously wrong, so we rushed her straight to the vet who whisked her away to conduct a thorough examination under anaesthesia and were dispatched home to await a telephone call. When the call came, we were informed she had glaucoma, that the pressure in her eye was so great it could burst and emergency surgery was needed to remove the eye immediately.

Our vet had taken advice from a specialist at a dedicated veterinary ophthalmology referral clinic in Herefordshire, to ensure she was doing the right thing. Anyone with an adored pet will understand the panic you feel and we were anxious to collect her post-op and bring her back once the vet deemed it safe. That evening our little girl was home, still sleepy and bandaged, accompanied by a load of tablets, with a follow-up appointment the next morning. We hovered like a couple of birds hatching an egg, probably irritating the hell out of her as she simply wanted to be left alone to sleep. Once assured she was ok, we left her to do just that. By Boxing Day (26th December) she was back to normal, running around like nothing had happened.

You've just got to admire dogs and their ability to recover and get on with life. Any human would have spent a week in bed, whingeing about the pain and moaning about the unfairness of it all!

Of course, Maisie's doggie insurance maxed out, so she was told to behave herself and not give us any more frights or cause to swell the vets' coffers further for at least twelve months. So far, so good!

In Need of a New TV

Prior to leaving for France, we'd decided it might be time to update our TV and other media at Les Hirondelles, but not to do anything rash ... just conduct an investigation to see what was out there. This necessitated a visit to one of the UK's large electrical stores for a bit of a mooch. The nearest one to us appears to have floor space bigger than your average football pitch. It's a dangerous place to be, wandering around shiny modern appliances that seem to do things your old stuff at home hasn't a clue about.

"What are you doing? I've been wandering around looking for you for half an hour. We're not here to look at washing machines," says a frustrated Rob.

"I know, but just look at this. Miles better than our old thing. It looks gorgeous and it's got three AAAs for economy!"

"Yeah, well, you can think about new washing machines, fridges and God knows what else when we've won the lottery."

"Huh. That's never going to happen. We never take part in it!"

Back where we should be, in the media area, we spent time gazing at the picture on an array of TVs bigger than the wall of our house, then moved onto the audio section where Rob likes to play by messing with stuff, usually switching on things which burst into life and threaten to damage the eardrums of anyone standing in the car park.

We eventually cast our eyes on a small, flat-screen, 'does everything but make the tea' TV. It was on special offer by supplying a sound bar as a companion gizmo. A nice man talked us through it, though I'm one of those people who really takes no notice of the fancy tech talk and is happy as long as it switches on and works as it should. The tech talk continued as we asked for advice about needing a satellite box, explaining it was for our house in France, which had a satellite dish. He agreed it was essential. As always, our 'not being rash' attitude was dead and buried as we headed off armed with said flat-screen TV and satellite box, to which was added an up-to-date, compatible DVD player. Well, it was a bargain!

I'm always amazed by technology and what things can do nowadays. I often wonder what my parents would think of it all if they were to be spirited back into this modern world of ours. Their first taste of modernity came in the guise of a stereogram. A monstrosity of a thing the size of a wardrobe which contained TWO speakers, a turntable with three speeds, a radio and a space to secure your few vinyl albums (LPs in old language) for safekeeping. It stood next to our first colour television, which was also a cumbersome object with a small screen and a massive back encasing everything which made it work.

I remember being flabbergasted when my parents bought a transistor radio. I quickly adopted it, as it was small enough for me to smuggle into bed at night, using the huge dial to locate Radio Luxemburg or pirate radio Caroline which broadcast from a boat bobbing around in international waters, both of which played all the latest pop music, albeit between the intermittent hiss, crackle and loss of signal. It also spent time, on Sundays, in the bathroom (bath night before school the next day), when the BBC finally caught on that youngsters were not interested in listening to 'old people's music' and launched Radio One. I'd stay in the bath for the entire *Pick of the Pops* (chart show). By the time it finished, the bathwater was freezing. No matter, as the bathroom was cold enough to store ice cream. Central heating was an unknown luxury in council housing back then. How times change.

My only complaint about tech is the speed with which it progresses. It always involves buying new kit to keep pace and I swear those brainy boffins in Silicon Valley and elsewhere invent all sorts, but the multi-billionaire bosses drip-feed it ensuring we have to keep digging deep. At least Rob and I are disciplined enough to hang onto our stuff until it becomes almost obsolete. My new phone is a case in point, but more of that later.

27

Making it to St Omer

As is generally the case, our overnight stop was to be in St Omer, but firstly we had to negotiate the Pet Reception and the pedantic staff at the Tunnel. I admit to being nervous about using the pet passports for the first time. A refusal would land us in deep *merde*. We'd thrown all our eggs into the Pet Passport basket and had chosen not to back them up with the Health Certificate.

We approached the counter and the smiley young lady. I beamed back at her believing it might help. She microscopically scanned the passports, slowly going through each page and then called over a supervisor. "Here we go." I whispered to Rob who gave me a hard look and raised his eyebrows. I tried to appear relaxed and confident, but it was a really anxious moment, as I held my breath awaiting the decision. There was a nod of consent. I couldn't hide the relief and headed to the car, clutching the windscreen sticker of approval while punching the air in glee. Rob remained his usual calm self, but I knew he'd had a slight wobble of concern while awaiting the result and was happy that the matter was settled in our favour. The dogs were congratulated on their reinstated French citizenship and we celebrated the fact we'd never have to fork out on fees for the Health Certificate ever again.

On every occasion we've used them since that first time, our egress out and re-entry into the UK has resulted in the supervisor being summoned. On one occasion, they actually laughed, saying they'd never seen such untidy and messy handwriting, complaining that the French was difficult to decipher. How is that our fault? I doubt our French vet would take kindly to us asking him to improve his cursive scribble. On our latest visit, the rabies jab expiry date was stated to be incorrect. It wasn't, we checked. We now expect this supervisory scrutiny and puzzlement each time we proffer them, with more nit-picking to find a non-fault in order to justify the staff's existence. Oh well, such is life.

At the Fair

In St Omer that night, we surprisingly stumbled upon an enormous funfair while walking the dogs before bed. The quiet squares were full of flashing lights and blazing colours. A confusion of loud pop music swirled into the cold night air, accompanied by the thrum of generators and machinery as they kept stomach-churning rides spinning in the air or swirling around at ground level, the occupant's decibel-busting screams adding to the hullaballoo. We strolled slowly through the melee of stalls to avoid tripping over the thick cables which snaked across the walkways, passing people stuffing themselves on a year's worth of sugar provided by several large sweet stalls, the length of your average articulated lorry. I'd never seen so much cloyingly sweet stuff in one place, even if it did look pretty with its rainbow bright colours. I began to feel my tooth enamel screaming!

The fair was sheer pandemonium and Maisie was finding it difficult. The unfamiliar noises emanating from the stalls and rides, particularly on her blind side, were beginning to scare her. Teddy, on the other hand, couldn't have cared less. He spent his time sniffing the air as the aroma of sausages cooking on the hot dog stalls assaulted his nostrils, appealing to his abiding love of food. We had to drag him past a couple where he yearned to linger to see what might come his way. After deciding we'd finally had enough, needing to remove Maisie from her scary surroundings and Teddy from foodie torture, we left the populace to their revelry and headed back to the hotel. We also needed an early night. There would be little time to laze in bed the following morning. It was up and out early to continue onwards towards Les Hirondelles.

Family Fun on the Snow

We arrived at the house a day before our daughter and her family were due. Venturing inside was like walking into a deep freeze, so coats and scarves remained firmly in place until a log fire was roaring and radiators had remembered how to work and thaw out the house. It didn't take long before the frigid air was replaced by warmth, all our unpacking was done, water was flowing happily within the pipes and hot food was gently digesting as we snuggled down for the evening.

The next day, we were looking forward to welcoming the family. However, plans went slightly awry due to flight delays with our daughter texting to explain they'd be arriving much later than expected and not to bother providing dinner. They had decided to eat at the airport rather than remain staring at the departures board for hours, waiting to see 'delayed' replaced by 'boarding'. It was after ten at night before we finally heard the car pull up outside, disgorging two weary adults and two sleepy children from the warmth of its interior into the dark night and a wall of face-slapping cold. After a struggle to settle two, now fully awake and excited little girls into bed, the adults lingered awhile, enjoying a drink and a chat before we all headed up the spiral staircase and the house fell silent.

The following day we had an early start. Our daughter and family left after breakfast to book the girls into ski school and to rent skis and boots. After clearing the breakfast mayhem, Rob and I finally headed off to join them, buying our ski passes while I worried whether my old knees would stand up to yet another year on the slopes. As a precaution, I had a pocketful of painkillers and pulled on a strong knee support under my ski pants.

Before climbing on the first ski lift of the holiday, we lingered for a while to observe our little granddaughters in ski school. The youngest was placed in 'Ourson' (Bear Cub), the name ESF (*Ecole Ski de France*) denotes the group where little ones with no skiing experience are accommodated. There is nothing quite like observing these tiny children trying to balance on the alien things attached to their strange boots. Taking a tumble never seems to hurt as they struggle to their feet, occasionally requiring the assistance of the ski instructor, just to do it all again, over and over until they get the hang of it. It's amazing the speed at which their confidence and ability grow. It's not long before a line of little people are snaking down the nursery slope behind the instructor who is trying to stop them from bowling off at speed by reminding them how to stop safely. Many don't, catapulting into the back of their waiting group and sending them toppling like a line of dominoes. They're soon back on their feet and off again, zig-zagging downhill in organised chaos. In the meantime, our seven-year-old was placed in 'Flocon' (Snowflake) and was off on the bigger slopes, using button and chair lifts and negotiating a baby slalom course. It's not going to be long before both completely outdo their ageing grandparents!

Rob and I have our favourite runs, but the weather had been extraordinary, with blazing sunshine and high temperatures, so snow cover was poor and not all the slopes were open. However, the snowmaking was extensive and higher up, the snow was great. My knee held up and my face managed to avoid making contact with the snow, though Rob did manage a couple of wipeouts. My courage made a break for it when I found myself perched at the top of a very steep run consisting of patches of ice interspersed with clumps of snow. I hovered at the top on wobbly legs, eyeing the drop. Rob launched over the edge, shouting "wimp" as a parting shot in my direction — probably revenge for the time I laughed at him as he lay flat out on the snow with a ski heading downhill without him.

Of course, I had to prove him wrong, held my breath and went for it. It wasn't elegant and not exactly the best example of skiing, but I slid down safely with much huffing and puffing and a celebratory shout as I joined my cheeky husband at the bottom. Just to prove a point and with confidence overflowing, I did it all again, twice, still lacking some of the necessary style and panache of those who have been born on skis, but bloody thrilled I'd conquered it without looking like a real twit!

The week flew by. We'd enjoyed an Ibiza-style clubbing session, supping hot chocolate as a DJ played cool sounds to skiers and boarders who had stopped at *La Parapente*, one of the on-slope restaurants. A group of teens loved the vibe, dancing about in the late afternoon sunshine in their cumbersome ski boots. I was tempted to join in but left them to it as Rob and I headed to the bottom to pick up the grandchildren from ski school and to meet up with their parents.

Our regular *après ski* took us to a local bar where some of the ski instructors meet at the end of the day. It's a small, cosy little place, its walls covered in hundreds of comments, written in black marker pen from customers who wished to let everyone know what a great time they'd had, expressing their feelings with hand-drawn smiley faced emojis, hearts and scribbled messages. The floor space, filled with a few high tables and bench seating, provides somewhere to sit while tucking into a pizza or light snack. A small bar completes the interior. The friendly owners have created a welcoming spot for families, dogs, friends, neighbours and visitors like us. No longer total strangers, we're always on the receiving end of a smile and a friendly greeting each time we pop in. With a great selection of good music playing, it's also the ideal setting for a couple of beers or a *vin chaud*, putting energy back into tired legs before we all head back to the house for dinner to do it all again the next day, weather permitting.

As many families readied to depart for home, their half-term at an end, the resort celebrated Friday night with a torchlight procession from the ski instructors. High above, the mountains silhouetted against the clear night sky, tiny specks of light appeared, slowly snaking down the lengthy piste, growing steadily larger as they neared the spectators who welcomed them back with applause and cheering. With music provided by a DJ at the foot of the slope, a firework display lit up the night sky with a festival of colour, reflecting across the snow and illuminating the trees. The night was cold and clear, the crowd snuggled inside their winter attire as everyone enjoyed the spectacle. The DJ continued playing his tunes as the last rocket fizzled out, with many folk remaining to dance for a while in the open air, singing along to popular songs and generally having a great time. We stayed too, lapping up the atmosphere until hunger started to bite and our feet started to feel the effect of enjoying a boogie on a dancefloor made of snow.

We waved our little family off the next morning, unbelievably proud of our little granddaughters who had been awarded their medals for achieving the required standard in ski school. With their ESF booklets completed and validated, they can both move to the next stage when they return to the slopes once more.

I always feel a little lost once they've all left. The house is no longer filled with their voices and frequent laughter. I also miss the love provided by two small humans who give the best hugs and say the funniest things. What I don't miss is the clutter; the hallway heaped with six pairs of snow boots, six pairs of ski boots, plus discarded hats, gloves, ski jackets and backpacks. The skis remain in the cars.

Tidying up following this whirlwind consisting of two lively children and their parents began in earnest the next day. The hallway, no longer looking like a badly organised ski wear jumble sale, was still in need of a broom and mop to deal with the escaped detritus from the soles of boots, plus the snowy puddles and muddy paw marks provided by Maisie and Teddy trailing in and out. Let's not forget the odd pine cone either, gifted by Teddy who treats such things as a ball, throwing it about as it sheds bits of itself all over the floor!

Tidying up becomes a voyage of discovery. "Are you sure you've got everything?" said I as they left. "Yes," they said. No, they hadn't! Something always goes astray.

One year our daughter remembered she'd left her passport in the ski hire shop where she'd used it as a guarantee against the rental equipment. The shop assistant had forgotten to return it and our daughter had forgotten it was there. Rob was nominated as courier, collected the passport and safely delivered it to Nice airport where our panicking daughter was finally able to board her flight home.

On another occasion, it was her driving licence. Thankfully, this didn't involve a journey to Nice, so it was stowed safely in a card pocket in the purse I used exclusively for euros. It was well hidden and I completely forgot it was there; a case of out of sight, out of mind, leaving me with no recollection of its whereabouts. She swore we'd got it, we swore we hadn't, she couldn't find it, we couldn't find it and it stayed that way for months until I was having a tidy up, clearing out our 'holiday' files and associated stuff to discover it exactly where I'd stowed it months earlier. A 'told you so' greeted my phone call.

I've found items of clothing, kids' hair bobbles, the odd earring and, regularly, crayons or pens lurking under sofas or beds. All are retrieved, returned or put away. Nowadays, I'm over the moon the children are no longer obsessed with stickers!

Frustration and Joy

Our new TV gear was installed once peace had returned to the house and Rob had time to do the job. He fiddled around with the satellite box and the menus found on-screen, none of which made any sense as we haven't got WiFi and therefore Netflix or any other streaming channel. All we wanted to find were a few standard UK TV channels. It didn't matter how many times we yelled at our new, very clever TV, it took no notice.

After a couple of hours of total frustration, foul tempers and a lot of bad language, Rob resorted to telephoning the helpline with a nice lady talking him through the procedure, there being no need for the satellite box which had been considered essential by our not so knowledgeable shop assistant. We simply had to connect directly to the satellite dish, which pleased the TV no end, producing a huge list of familiar and not-so-familiar channels and navigation screens we could understand. The defunct satellite box was secured back in its box to await return from whence it came.

Gilbert had remained at his home in Cannes for the duration of our stay, so we didn't catch up with him on this occasion, but the son of Albert and Simone was in residence for a couple of days allowing us to enquire after Simone. Thankfully, she was as well as she could be considering she was in her nineties. Our new neighbour didn't appear either, but Gaia, as always, popped down to see our dogs, enjoying a quick sniff around, before heading off to continue her explorations elsewhere.

We continued with the skiing for a couple of half days, ending each afternoon with a visit to our usual bar where we'd met an English couple and their dog the week previously. It's quite rare to run into Brits in our ski resort as most head for the big boys further north, so meeting a British couple always piques our curiosity. They were as curious as we were and on that first meeting, we discovered much about each other. They had decided to retire and grab life by the horns, renting out their home in the UK, choosing to live on a houseboat in the Netherlands and leading an exciting life exploring the waterways. They also had an apartment not far from where we were sitting. We, on the other hand, had done nothing quite so brave, but they were impressed by the amount of travel we'd enjoyed in earlier days and the fact we'd actually met at school, wound up getting married and managed to stay that way. We got along famously and agreed to meet them again during our final week, when the conversation flowed and a new friendship was born. We agreed to stay in touch, swapping emails and finding each other on Facebook. We're happily still in touch and will meet up again when back next winter.

When not on the slopes or making new friends, we spent our time walking the dogs or relaxing with a book, sitting on the balcony in the sunshine, wrapped in a jacket or fleece. At night we'd curl up in front of the fire and watch the news on the TV, horrified by the reports that Russia had invaded Ukraine after promising they wouldn't. Across that week, the reports became more horrific. The deaths of innocents and the desperation of those fleeing the indiscriminate bombardment of their homes, clutching what few possessions they could carry, had me in tears. Today, Rob and I still wonder at the madness of a regime, run by a despot, who values life so little.

As the end of the week approached, the dogs were taken to the vet for their passport necessities and I cleaned the house, sadly packing our belongings knowing we wouldn't be back until the summer.

We left to undertake our two-day journey home the following day.

28

Interesting, Spooky and Ouch!

The weather decided to show a miserable face as we headed north, stopping overnight in a lovely chalet hotel we often use situated in the Franche-Comté, atop a ridge standing at 343 metres (1,125 feet) above sea level and called *Mont Roland*. The area provides some brilliant walks for us and our dogs through woodland or across large, open expanses of grass, with extensive views towards the Jura massive to the east and the plains of the river Saône to the north and west.

The hotel sits within a tiny commune of a few houses and a lovely old church with an impressively large and imposing building next to it. Travelling along the road towards the hotel and the commune, the route is lined on one side by seven towering stone crosses placed equidistant to one another. We initially thought they might be memorials to those who had perished during the two world wars, but none bore any references, so, eventually, we asked the owner of the hotel for an explanation. He told us that the crosses represent the first seven Stations of the Cross, which meant little to Rob and me as we're neither Catholic nor particularly religious. It was explained there are fourteen stations in all, each representing a stage that Jesus experienced before his crucifixion.

Being endlessly curious, particularly when it comes to the history of places we visit, I needed to find out more. Further research to find information on the history of this place threw up some fascinating details, a few of which might be of interest to some of you, believers or not. I've kept it short for those who aren't.

Legend has it that the first chapel was consecrated here in the fourth century by St Martin and was succeeded by a second chapel erected by Roland 'le Preux', a nephew of Charlemagne, from whom the 'Mount' takes its name.

The sanctuary of Notre Dame du Mont Roland is one of the oldest places of pilgrimage in the area and is on one of the routes of the Camino de Santiago de Compostela, which is some walk!

Several miracles are said to have taken place during the 1600s. A few were investigated and acknowledged. I've read about the miracles and frankly, can't understand what all the fuss was about. Surely you can recover from a mild illness without it being attributed to divine intervention.

The Benedictines established a priory here which they kept for nine hundred years and were driven out during the French Revolution. The building was sold. The Jesuits who bought and restored it in 1843, were expelled in 1901 and the building was auctioned. They were allowed to return and stayed until 1961. Its current incarnation is a retreat, hosting any who wish to escape the world and commune with the Almighty if that's your thing.

The Stations of the Cross were erected in 1893.

Pilgrimages continue to this day, including one held on 2nd August each year since 1859. It attracts up to three thousand pilgrims.

It seems the place has been sacked, renovated and battered by conflicts, including the smashing of the stained glass window caused by shock waves from American bombardment during WWII. It has been rebuilt, repaired, bought and sold, with its history involving kings, archbishops, lords, leaders, mayors, soldiers, saints and sinners. We hadn't a clue we'd been staying somewhere quite so significant.

Aside from all the history, the hotel is just a nice place to stay as the host is friendly and always makes a huge fuss of his doggie guests as well as their accompanying humans. After what is a good dinner, we always take the dogs for their evening constitutional around the locality before bed.

On this particular dark night, huddled in our coats under low clouds, we were returning from our walk, anxious to retreat to the warmth of our room. The lights around the sanctuary pierced the darkness, with the chapel illuminated by fluorescent uplighters. We were surrounded by total silence except for the sound of our footfalls and the patter of paws. Suddenly, for a brief moment, reflected in the cloud before us, the misty image of the church spire appeared. It looked quite eerie seeing it there, hovering above our heads, especially when you consider where we were. I managed to quickly take a couple of shots of this phenomenon with my mobile phone before the image slowly dissolved leaving no trace it had ever existed. Strangely, once home and having downloaded all my photos onto my computer, I've never been able to find those particular shots. I put it down to accidentally deleting them, but the whole experience was a bit like something from the *Twilight Zone*.

Moving on from the weird and wonderful, another nightly dog walk at the same location a year earlier resulted in my dramatic face-plant performance onto the gravel slabs outside the hotel. Maisie was off her lead and I'd only glanced across at her for a split second to reassure myself she was still alongside, failing to see the small raised kerb stone lying in wait. It all happened so quickly! I had no time to put out my hands so my face slammed into the floor. Thankfully, I managed to turn it slightly before impact, so happily my nose avoided being flattened like a losing boxer after twelve rounds. Rob dashed to my rescue while I attempted to restart my breathing and not to be a crybaby. Once back in our room after Rob had gently escorted me there, preventing any further mishaps, a tentative glance in the mirror and a fingertip exploration of the 'sore bit', confirmed my cheek was starting to balloon nicely.

I had no intention of arriving bruised and battered at breakfast the next morning, further wounding my dignity as any enquiries would force me to admit what a dimwit I'd been. Nor was I willing to look like the mother of a Cabbage Patch Kid (Fat-faced children's doll), drawing curious stares from the general public. Preventative measures were urgently required, so Rob was immediately dispatched to find out if the hotel had a medical box. He returned bearing soothing lotions, antiseptics and a bag of ice. Ample amounts of ointments were applied, pain relief medications swallowed and shivering endured, while holding a bag of ice to my cheek for half an hour—all resulting in an enquiry-free breakfast, due to scant evidence of my fall except for a small bruise and a tiny bit of swelling on my cheekbone.

Oh, before you all ask, alcohol had nothing to do with it!

Once home, our satellite box was returned, but the store refused to refund the money, insisting they'd only provide a credit note as we'd had the item for too long. It was explained that whoever sold it to us had been aware of where it was going, why it was going and when it was going, assuring us all would be well. He got that wrong!

PART V

SUMMERTIME JOURNEYS

29

Travels South

Our Discovery had been in for a final check to ensure everything was glued, screwed and nailed down and had been 'valeted' by some pleasant guys in a convenient location a few miles from us. A sparkling clean vehicle and the reassurance that nothing would drop off it, fall to bits or stop working was a great comfort considering the inside was stuffed with dog food, a cool box-type fridge, luggage, all our camping gear and God knows what else. I worried about the ability of the suspension to cope with all the weight.

The dogs were unhappy that their space for spreading out had been restricted, due to the lowering of a section of the back seat. They were happy, however, that their own bedding, which filled the remaining space, rested atop sleeping bags strewn underneath. This provided added height for them to see the world pass by from the windows and added comfort as they sank into a cocoon of softness. Keeping them safe is always uppermost in our minds when travelling, so they were securely attached to their doggie seat belts and promised plenty of breaks for water, a treat and time to pee or poo.

Gaps behind seats were filled, door pockets stuffed and the central bit cluttered with charging cables, mobile phones, Rob's sunglasses, glasses and his wallet. It would soon contain a pile of fuel receipts and other rubbish. I sensed it wouldn't be long before he lost something for it to be discovered later down the side of the driver's seat, on the floor, in a coat pocket or stashed underneath a dog!

My handbag is always stationed in the footwell for instant access. It contains multiple pockets containing all my essentials and other bits and bobs I've not seen for years, but at least I know where it is—well, most of it. I admit rooting around in it is a voyage of discovery, sometimes finding a lipstick I've not seen for ages, the odd Covid face mask, assorted pens or a jumble of tablets for several types of temporary ailments. Rob is mystified by it all but often benefits from what I can conjure up when he's in need. He does possess the male equivalent. A nice tan leather satchel that he occasionally uses for the storage of non-essentials then leaves hanging in the bedroom or as an additional piece of luggage, which lies in the boot of the car. Perhaps he wouldn't misplace stuff quite so often if he used his own bag. It would also prevent him from asking me to carry his essentials in mine!

Our first night in St Omer was uneventful, apart from the fact that the restaurant was closed and we were forced to locate food elsewhere. With multiple restaurants close by, we were spoiled for choice and eventually wandered into the first one we'd come across, after walking for half an hour investigating all the others. We left after a very expensive dinner, throwing caution to the wind with our usual: "Well it is the first night of our holiday, so let's spoil ourselves."

When planning our trip through France towards Les Hirondelles, great consideration is given to our overnight stays. Across the years we've discovered the delightful and not so delightful. Thankfully, it has been a rare event to encounter any who convinced us never to cross that particular threshold again. Initially, full of energy and urgency, we would leave home in the middle of the night and be halfway through France before stopping for food and rest, completing our journey the following day. Knowing our time was limited because of full-time work commitments, getting there as soon as possible meant we could squeeze in maximum time in the mountains. We also left at the last possible minute, aiming for enough time back at home to benefit from a modicum of sleep before commencing the daily grind the next day.

It wasn't long before we decided energy and urgency should be evicted in favour of taking a more leisurely journey, no longer involving a struggle to get out of bed at some ungodly hour and seeing large portions of France zip past the window at speed. From then on, we adopted a relaxed attitude towards our travels, taking time to reach our destination easily in three days and often, on return journeys, diverting to places we wished to explore, remaining for several days.

Lodging is booked before we leave the UK and care is taken to ensure it accepts our doggie companions, doesn't cost a fortune and appears to be of a reasonable standard. Many of these residences have become firm favourites and we often return to enjoy the atmosphere, food and area in which they are located.

Our second night fell into this category, staying in a large chalet-style *auberge* in the tiny village of Aranc, situated in the Ain department of the south-eastern Auvergne-Rhone Alpes. The village itself has nothing to mark it out as being of interest apart from its position in a remote spot high in the hills, surrounded by forests and farmland. Our journey, once leaving the autoroute, takes us away from civilisation and into a world of greenery, small farms and narrow winding roads. The twisting route soon takes on some height as the car is manoeuvred around a series of steep switchback turns, providing stunning views across a patchwork of fields and woodland as you progress upwards. The village lies atop a plateau, the highest point being the Col du Cendrier at 793 metres (2600 feet), just to the north.

Upon entering Aranc you will find yourself in the midst of a few houses, farm buildings, a church and the *auberge*. The village is also blessed with a fabulous *laiterie*, the counters filled with numerous and diverse types of cheeses, much of it produced from milk supplied by the ubiquitous cows in the surrounding fields. The hotel is very much in the Swiss chalet style and in summer, the large balcony and window boxes are adorned with clouds of bright red geraniums, adding to its appeal.

Dead opposite the hotel, beyond a green space with a central pathway and a few stone steps at its end, is the entrance to the quaint church. It's always a bit of a worry having a church within hearing distance as village churches in France seem to love clanging their bells, especially in the early morning, with many following Angelus, timing them to ring three times a day starting at 7.00 am. (Angelus is a Catholic devotion, said three times a day, morning, noon and night). However, local traditions might have bells ringing before 6.00 am or at midnight. An early night or a lie-in may be rudely interrupted unless you are deaf or using earplugs. Thankfully, this church avoided using its bells to act as an early morning wake-up alarm for local farmers.

I recently came across an amusing article linked to this, describing a growing problem. Urbanites buying weekend properties in an attempt to escape to the country, seemed to have besieged village mayors with formal complaints about noise and smells. Cockerels crowing, ducks quacking, geese honking, tractors moving, bells ringing and farmyard smells are just a few of those mentioned. It became so bad that in response, the government voted in a new law, which formally protects France's rural heritage–meaning it makes it more difficult to complain and helps to protect the character of small villages and ancient customs. The minister in charge of rural life stated that people living in the countryside will now have to accept nuisances such as cowbells, cow droppings, grasshopper chirps and early morning tractors! This man obviously has a great sense of humour.

That night we chose to eat dinner on the terrace, it being pleasantly warm, even if the skies looked a little grey. A couple of gentlemen sitting at a table to the side offered a warm greeting and smiled at our dogs who, as usual, had made themselves comfortable under the table. At breakfast the next morning, we had the opportunity to chat with them again as we were leaving. They were a fabulous couple, one of which was marvellously camp, chatty and full of smiles, his partner quieter and more considered. They spoke some English and were delighted they'd had the chance to speak to some real British natives and proceeded to tell us, gushing with enthusiasm, about the Queen's Platinum Jubilee.

"Oh, your reine, your Queen, she eez wonderful! We watch ze Jubilee on ze

TV. It was spectaculaire, magnifique! We 'ave never seen zis before. In France, zis is never 'appening. Ow we weesh we 'ad a reine!"

(One wonders how they responded to our Queen's state funeral!)

It was quite a revelation to meet two French citizens who were so keen on the way us Brits 'put on a show'. Apart from their obvious delight and fascination with all things royal, we did glean they lived in Paris and were on their way to the Cote d'Azure for a two-week holiday. We wished them a *très bonnes vacances* leaving them to finish their breakfast and wishing we'd had more time to linger in the company of these lovely guys.

As Rob loves strong cheeses, including the stinky varieties which smell like sweaty feet, once our overnight bags and dogs were stowed in the car, we trotted across to the laiterie to inspect their wares. Amongst this tasty feast of flavours and consistencies, I needed to ensure we took away a few of my favourites too; those small round *crottins* of goat cheese, of which this place has many, their creamy rounds covered in a variety of complementary coatings. The lady serving was open to supplying Rob with small samples of cheese while I was busy pondering my other favourite items, their homemade yoghurts, displayed in an array of tiny jars. I've never seen quite so many in one place. The rich, thick yoghurt rests on a layer of real fruit *coulis* in every possible flavour and, as 'live' yoghurt, they are not only good for you, they taste divine! We never leave Aranc without a hoard of the *laiterie's* offerings onboard.

A Bit of Science and SatNavs

Our journey took us in a south-easterly direction where we would eventually join the autoroute from Chambery to Grenoble. The first part of our journey was once again devoid of much human habitation except for a few lonely properties. Fields full of cows grazing happily on the lush grass were the only obvious signs of life for a while, except for the rare appearance of a passing car. We continued on, weaving through woodland whose branches formed a shady canopy above, the leaves filtering the sunlight into tiny shafts reflected on the road's surface. Eventually, the car plunged sharply downhill on another series of steep switchback turns, through a village whose homes are blessed with an amazing view of the valley below. At the foot lay the village of Tenay and the main road we would follow to Belley, then beyond towards the Col de Chat.

There's a reason I love travelling towards the Col. An uphill climb to the top will find you entering the Tunnel de Chat, nearly a mile long (1486 metres to be precise). In fact, it's two tunnels, one lying adjacent and slightly higher providing a safe route for cyclists and pedestrians while traffic uses the other. Although the tunnel is a bit of a thrill, it's leaving it that always makes me gasp as the view of Lac Bourget is revealed, lying in all of its 18 km (just over 11 miles) long, azure blue glory in the valley below, surrounded by the peaks of the Bauges mountains. Just around the sharp bend after leaving the tunnel, is a series of small restaurants and every time we venture this way, we stop for a short break, providing water for the dogs and a cooling beer for us as we chill in the shade and admire the dramatic scenery before us, partly obscured by the traffic entering or leaving the tunnel.

Lac Bourget is the largest natural lake in France and it's pretty deep. At its maximum, it reaches 145 metres (nearly 476 feet) but apart from this, it contains a rare phenomenon that occurs in only thirty-six lakes on the entire planet, fourteen of which occur in the USA and none at all in the UK.

I had cause to do a bit of research a couple of years ago after a visit to Lac Pavin, a crater lake in the Puy de Dome and the only other lake in France in which this phenomenon occurs. Information boards explained the lake was 'meromictic'. We hadn't a clue what that meant. Curiosity meant I needed to investigate. All the scientific, multi-syllabic gobbledygook completely flew over my head. Therefore I shall resort to the simplest and most basic explanation that us mere mortals can fathom, which you may want to impress your friends with.

In all other lakes (known as 'holomictic'), the waters mix naturally on a seasonal basis, top to bottom. Depending on the lake this can be once or several times a year. Therefore the water contains enough oxygen in its entirety to support fish and other organisms. In a 'meromictic' lake, water is oxygenated in the top layer, but only trace amounts are found in the deep and denser layer below, where no life, apart from some bacteria, can be sustained. The water never mixes, so sediments and gasses can build up for eons in this lower section. It seems that sometimes these may consist of carbon dioxide and other nasties. If this layer is disturbed by a large earthquake along the lake bed, for example, it is possible any poisonous gasses present can be forced to the surface and released into the air. This happened in Lake Nyos in Cameroon in 1986 where they were the cause of nearly 1,800 deaths amongst the local people who lived in near proximity to the lake and around 2,500 deaths of animals and birds. Examination proved a catastrophic release of carbon dioxide was to blame.

Lac Bourget, however, is safe for all normal human watery activity and I'm sure that gasses are monitored by those qualified to do such things, ensuring there is nothing noxious and deadly lurking in the deep. Therefore this lake contains several varieties of fish to keep anglers happy, a marina is situated on the lake at Aix les Bains to keep the boaters happy and swimming is allowed. So don't panic should you find yourself near the lake and in need of a refreshing dip to escape the heat.

On this occasion, the weather was particularly sweltering and we were loath to leave our shady corner, enveloped in overhanging trees and shrubs and sitting on stools at a tiny table. The dogs lay alongside, panting like steam trains, but they needed to move after being cooped up in the car and no doubt were in need of a pee. I checked the baking tarmac to ensure the dogs wouldn't burn their footpads as we crossed the road. A gravel pathway led us to where the land dropped steeply with nothing to interrupt the view apart from a few trees. It's a great spot for a photo as the panorama reveals itself without the nuisance of a main road getting in the way.

The blue lake shimmered in the sunshine, its surface scattered with the reflections from passing clouds above. Differing shades of green were shared between trees, shrubs and grassy banks, dotted here and there with the odd wildflower. Across the lake, on the far bank, Aix les Bains and its suburbs spilled down to the lake's edge, while behind, the Bauge mountains hovered, appearing grey-blue in the haze. We lingered for a short time taking photos, but needed to remove ourselves from the sun's rays which were beginning to make our skin scream. Respite was temporarily sought and found at the entrance of the pedestrian tunnel where the shade was welcoming and the air beautifully cool. After five minutes of bliss, we knew we had to leave and head back to the car, the inside of which was now as hot as hell, so the air con was turned to the maximum as we waved goodbye to Lac Bourget and headed onwards for our final four-hour journey towards our little French home.

The Trouble With SatNavs

The 'D' road heading from Monestier to Sisteron is a joy. It presents some spectacular views meandering as it does around a multitude of bends towards the Col de la Croix Haute, remarkable for being the site of an attack on a German convoy by the resistance in WW2. A monument here bears tribute to the resistance members who died. Thereafter the road heads downhill and threads its way through a series of picturesque villages and a valley with acres of apple trees in industrial quantities. On a good day, we can negotiate the 106 km (66 miles) in a couple of hours and enjoy a quick snack and dog walk along the way.

However, this was summer, it was a Saturday and it was August. Joined by hundreds of other Europeans in a variety of vehicles, including the ever-popular camper vans which appear to have a speed limiter set to 'oh so slow', it wasn't long before everything came to a standstill. One small comfort was the absence of huge lorries and tankers, the authorities having banned them from the route over this busy weekend. Mind you, it made not one jot of difference to our international traffic queue as we crawled along at a snail's pace. On one occasion several years ago, it took eight hours to complete this portion of the journey, so you're probably wondering why we chose to travel when we did. Unfortunately for us, commitments at home contrived to put us in this position.

Diverting around it all is impossible on the way up to the Col, with roads heading off to meet a village with a dead end or the wall of a mountain. Beyond the Col and quite a distance further on, some traffic will turn off towards Gap to encounter yet another horrendous jam of motor vehicles. In the past, we have occasionally been held up because of a minor accident, breakdown or found ourselves stuck behind a snowplough if the winter weather is misbehaving, but as these occurrences were outside of the holiday season, the light traffic managed to manoeuvre around the obstruction.

It's not all bad. One happy delay occurred a couple of years ago while driving to Les Hirondelles with my friend. We were surprised to be stopped and held up for two hours, the road being closed to await the Tour de France, inconveniently needing to peddle its way across to access some precipitous route on the other side. At least on that occasion, a buzz of excitement was in the air as we left our car, had pleasant conversations with fellow travellers and were able to witness a stream of world-class cyclists in Lycra stream past.

In traffic jams, our sat nav is totally bewildered, failing to understand why we want to leave the only direct route and locate what we call a 'rat run'. I often lose my temper with the thing as it starts being obnoxious and stubborn. Mind you, it doesn't help when your husband makes a one-digit error entering a French postcode, which he did a while back, the result of which was our arrival at a farmyard, miles from anywhere. Tempers were frayed and an additional hour was added to our journey to get where we wanted to be. He has been careful to not repeat this digit failure since.

Our Discovery is a pensioner in vehicular terms, our sat nav is now an unSATisfactory nav, failing to recognise new roads and suffering electronic dementia. We could update it, but it would be cheaper to launch our own satellite. Google Maps are our 'go-to', but even that doesn't help when trying to find teeny-weeny routes through unnamed places with no road numbers.

These misdirections, mishaps and muddles convinced me a good old-fashioned, up-to-date road atlas was the answer. In our current situation, this new purchase proved invaluable as I squinted at the appropriate page, locating small roads that squiggled their way through the open countryside roughly in our direction of travel. Rob admits I've always been good at reading a map. This is probably due to the Outward Bound course I was sent on at age sixteen where they dropped us in the middle of Snowdonia with an Ordinance Survey map and expected us to safely hike our way back to the residential centre without getting lost or dying of exposure.

Armed with reading glasses and a road atlas, I took on the role of sat nav, issuing directions like a co-driver on a cross-country rally, only much slower of course, successfully guiding Rob through tiny hamlets, over streams and past farmers' fields, staying roughly parallel to the clogged up main route, with an occasional glimpse of the slow-moving vehicles in the far distance. Our rat run was totally deserted, except for a farmer and his tractor who appeared surprised to see us. We finally re-joined the queue a short distance from our destination having saved considerable time as well as preventing the onset of boredom, frustration and the burning of expensive fuel while getting nowhere.

30

Noisy Neighbours

A t the house, on our first full day, I once more bemoaned the fact that weeds and grass had made themselves comfortable and shrubs had flourished in our absence. My back began to ache in anticipation. Apart from this regular chore, little else needed urgent attention, so we settled into a happy rhythm of pleasing ourselves with how we spent our days.

We'd noticed that the property housing our young neighbour and his family appeared deserted. All evidence of habitation was removed, the house shuttered with no dog popping down to say hello. Gilbert and Annie were around, so that was the obvious place to start. Gilbert confirmed the family had moved out and were renting a house in our local village. It seems our presumption they had bought their previous dwelling as a renovation project was completely incorrect. It had been a long-term rental. No matter. We were sure we'd bump into the family and their dog at some point when out shopping, though it was sad that our commune had reduced in numbers once more.

Another observation concerned Gabriel and Marsella's house below. Long empty after the elderly farmers had passed away, it had been bought by a non-local family three years ago and set to become their holiday home. The property would make a beautiful residence but needed a lot of work inside and out to bring it up to scratch. As mentioned earlier, the sounds of demolishing emanating from the interior appeared to indicate they were bashing down walls, but since then, their enthusiasm seems to have waned somewhat. In our absence, we always hoped we'd return to see some progress, but nothing appears to change. It seems the house remains as it was and the family are never seen, apart from summertime when they suddenly appear with their four dogs in tow, stay a couple of hours, and then disappear once again.

One afternoon, after a lengthy morning walk with the dogs, we were settled comfortably on the balcony enjoying some downtime under the shade of the canopies. Rob was snoozing and I was happily reading a lengthy tome on my Kindle. Gilbert and Annie were having their afternoon siesta indoors and it seemed, those currently resident in the commune, were doing the same. The only noises to disturb this somnolent post-lunch were the chirruping of birds, the faint burble of the river Verdon and the occasional sound of a car heading along the distant valley road.

All was peaceful and my eyelids were getting heavy, but any thoughts of a quick nap were abandoned when a car arrived on the road below, emptying itself of the family and their dogs. Much loud chatter followed as the lady of the family and her grown daughter headed away from their holiday home and spent the next two hours (I kid you not) chatting with someone they knew further along, the conversation taking place on a bend that squeezes the tiny road around the corner between two buildings. In the meantime, the husband pulled an old, petrol-driven strimmer from his car and proceeded to trim the weeds springing up at the base of the wall around their property. The noise was enough to rattle teeth. Gilbert, obviously rudely awakened, rushed onto his balcony to see what was going on, glanced across at us, and shrugged his shoulders while shaking his head in disbelief. The ear-splitting noise went on for quite a while before the man placed the strimmer back in the car and went to join his wife and daughter.

This rather intrusive and noisy interlude brought back memories of the time we were sanding down the old balcony. The clock had reached 12.30 pm and we'd nearly finished, but a rather strange lady we'd previously observed acting a tad weirdly dashed into the road some distance away and began to scream at us in rapid French about the noise, shouting it was "DEJEUNER, DEJEUNER!" We stopped immediately, not wishing to upset anyone. Daniel's wife just happened along the road at this point and went to calm the situation, probably informing her we didn't know any better because we were English. Both disappeared from view, but a couple of minutes later, the lady reappeared, convincing us she was a bit peculiar by walking into the middle of the road, performing a mock curtsey while pulling some rather strange faces aimed directly at me, the meaning of which were abundantly clear. Thankfully we've not seen her in years, so presume she's safely locked away somewhere receiving treatment.

We also managed to upset the lady who lives next door to Gabriel and Marsella's house by carrying out another sanding job, this time on a Sunday. She wasn't pleased. We gathered this when she stood chatting to a member of the community police and pointed directly at us in a rather accusatory way. Before being hauled off to be fined or imprisoned, we stopped all work and didn't resume until the following morning.

All this happened in our very early days of French house ownership, when still in that English frame of mind where noisy DIY is done without the need to clock watch. You know what it's like, you grab a quick sarnie (sandwich) and a cuppa, guzzle them down in record time and continue working until the job is done or you decide you've had enough

Nowadays, thoroughly educated in French lunchtime etiquette and content by participating in joining the very long lunch break, we have been accepted as well-behaved Brits and have attracted no unpleasant attention since.

31

Sheep, Shepherds and Wolves

Summer in the mountains is usually hot, the mornings presenting blue, cloudless skies which may attract a few cotton wool puffs of cloud as afternoon approaches, blown in on gentle breezes. These days often encourage an attack of laziness where the only exercise is a saunter down to the bins. After a day of doing nothing, my Fitbit failed to award a star for achieving a suitable step count and I needed to do something to gain its approval. This usually involves dragging Rob out and about for a hike. He's amenable to doing so as long as it doesn't involve struggling up near-vertical slopes, in rarified air, to the top of a mountain.

This particular summer, I dragged Rob all over the place, discovering places we'd never encountered before, where we were met with some real surprises, but our first day out was a much loved and familiar journey up to the Col d'Allos by car.

The route up is sinuous and steep, where barriers to stop a car from flying over the edge are rare. The road is so bad that it actually features on a website which describes the most dangerous roads in Europe and in this case, warns of bumps and steep drop-offs, further scaring the hell out of folks by saying it's not for the fainthearted. We have been up and down it so many times I've lost count, joined by countless others who also don't mind risking life and limb. In winter, the road is buried under snow and closed to traffic, the area swallowed by the area's ski domain. On this particular day, snow didn't figure at all as we arrived at the top of the Col in bright sunshine, with a warm breeze, lacking the slight chill that requires reaching for something to cover bare arms.

In summer, the Col and its surroundings get busy as it's a main route between the Ubaye Valley and the Verdon Valley. Many visitors stop, spending a moment to take in the spectacular views, with bikers and cyclists usually found posing for photos in front of the road sign which displays the altitude. Some individuals may venture further and follow one of the trails that snake off in various directions to disappear into the mountains.

When we arrived there appeared to be some kind of celebration going on at the top of a steep grassy slope. Rob and I have always admired the French for finding any excuse to set up a table or two, fill them with alcoholic beverages and have a bit of a ding-dong, but it was something we hadn't quite expected to see at 2,250 metres (7,380 feet).

At this time of year, sheep can be spotted across the whole area, moving freely from one fertile pasture to another. The shepherds live amongst them for months, finding shelter in *cabanes* (mountain cabins) if needed which are placed in sheltered spots within grazing areas. Their well-trained dogs guard the sheep, ready to attack any threat, be it an excited dog or a curious human. Notices are often placed to warn visitors against approaching and to keep dogs on leads.

A creature who would no doubt welcome a fat sheep on its menu also lurks within the Mercantour National Park, the beautiful and shy grey wolf. We were unaware of the story surrounding these creatures and the fact they inhabited the area, but had the opportunity to find out more when a few years ago we took a day's drive to the Col du Cayolle. At the top, a convenient hostelry supplied serious hikers with lodging and visitors with food and drinks. After ploughing through an enormous ham and cheese baguette each, we popped into the small information centre to discover walls adorned with photos of wolves and facts about the re-introduction of these animals.

A helpful and knowledgeable park ranger explained wolf numbers had drastically declined due to hunting and loss of habitat caused by human encroachment. In 1940 they were declared extinct across all of France. Then, in 1992, a pair of grey wolves were discovered in the Park having wandered across the border from Italy. This couple were responsible for establishing a population that has stretched across the whole of the Alps from north to south. Numbers are now around six hundred individuals.

It's a very divisive subject as conservationists and the public are in support of the wolf, but farmers and shepherds are most definitely not. Those in the south claim several thousand sheep are being lost annually. However, the Bern Convention, passed in 1979, was established to provide the wolf with protection, the French government making good by offering financial compensation for losses of stock due to wolf attacks. They also allow some culling if wolf attacks are frequent in a particular area or if populations are too large.

We asked our ranger how many wolves were actually found within the boundaries of the Mercantour and if he'd actually encountered any of our lupine friends up close. He answered in the affirmative, stating that rangers help with the monitoring of our local population, numbering around twenty to thirty in two small packs, largely roaming in the high mountains, remote and isolated. We didn't find out how many sheep were snatched but our local wolves have plenty of additional choices when hungry, preying on chamois, ibex, mouflon and wild boar. Today it seems sheep and wolf exist in an uneasy symbiosis, but we were thrilled to know the wolf had once more reclaimed the wild and rugged areas of the Mercantour, though a guest at Les Hirondelles swore she and her family saw a wolf, spying it from above as they travelled on the chairlift at Seignus a couple of summer's ago. Makes us think we'll have to keep a close eye on our pooches when out walking, just in case Mr Wolf fancies a quick snack!

On this occasion, the wolves were thankfully going about their business elsewhere as a huge flock of sheep had been herded together across the slope, well away from the road. We made sure that both Maisie and Teddy were securely attached to their leads to prevent any threats, such as being savaged by the guard dogs or shot by a shepherd. Mind you, Maisie doesn't like sheep and Teddy, after coming face to face with one, gave it a curious sniff and took no notice, but we would never, ever risk letting them roam free when sheep are about.

Rob held onto the dogs, standing on a raised bank, high above the road, as I trundled off to find out what was going on. I failed miserably as it seemed any celebration or simple shepherd gathering had ended. The sheep had returned to their wanderings, the shepherds had gone to join them and tables were being packed away. I was about to ask someone when a young motorcyclist, who had pulled up behind, caused a distraction by thrusting his phone at me, asking nicely in French if I'd take his photo. Of course I obliged, taking a few of him posing alongside his motorbike with the road sign displaying 'Col d'Allos, Alt 2,250 metres', clearly visible behind. By the time he'd thanked me, everyone concerned with the mountainside shindig had wandered off.

Returning to Rob after failing in my quest, we took a dog each and followed a fairly level path which wended its way across the top of the ridge. On one side, the land started to slope gently towards the road which snakes 17 kilometres (10.5 miles) down to Barcelonnette. The route on this side of the Col is also a very scary ride for those suffering from vertigo. Some of the drop-offs plunge into the Gorges de Bachelard where the road to the Col du Cayolle can be seen in its depths. It's also very narrow in places, so meeting a camper van approaching from the opposite direction can be the cause of a real stomach churn as your car squeezes past with wheels inches from the edge. I treated three of my friends to this trip, two of whom hate heights, but the views across to some very impressive mountain peaks proved an excellent distraction and they made it without too many scared whimpers.

Rob and I followed our pathway for an hour or so, revealing the top point of one of the ski lifts at the Tete du Vescal with Mount Seolane as a backdrop. The mountain is easily recognisable as it looks as though some large mythical creature took a spoon to its ridge and scooped out a small, but perfectly formed 'U' shape.

Up here you could walk for days, but it was way past lunchtime, so we turned back, grabbed the car and drove a little way to the *Refuge Col d'Allos* for a beer and a chill, sitting at an outside table under a sunny sky with uninterrupted views of the mountains before finally heading back to Les Hirondelles to enjoy a planned BBQ dinner that evening.

32

A Market for the Senses

It was Friday and market day. Wandering through the narrow streets, stuffed with stalls and people, turns out to be a real sensory experience. Let's start this trip by exercising your sense of smell. Aromas float in the air and pleasantly assault the nostrils as you wander past the cheese stalls, or perhaps one with a display of cured meats. Then the spice stall, always in a good spot by the old town wall, where you can't avoid the aromatic scent of the spicy and hot, the mellow and flavoursome or the *mélange* that makes up herbs de Provence.

Next is the artisan bread stall where huge loaves are cut and weighed into manageable pieces for people to take home. The smell of the fresh bread is homely and delicious and trying to resist buying is futile. The peppery waft of fat olives, pickled garlic, tapenades and other assorted delights will draw you in to select your choices from a colourful display on a stall opposite the spice stall. Once around the corner, passing through the old town gateway, you'll find yourself in a small car park, where stalls shelter under the shade of plane trees. Here your nose will detect a hint of the ocean, all made clear when you find yourself heading towards the van displaying a stunning array of fresh fish and seafood. Beyond this, if a meat eater, you'll be salivating at the scent of free-range chickens, guinea fowl and ham hocks, turning slowly on the rotisseries. If you arrive early, you may need to order, leaving your name, so you can pick it up once cooked. If you arrive late, you may be lucky and find a few still remaining, cooked and arranged in trays, ready to take back for lunch or dinner.

Then, outside the hotel bar, you'll find the headiest scent of all, for here is the lavender stall. The lavender oil is produced locally from the fragrant flowers harvested from the distillery's own fields. The pure oil is sold in small bottles and only needs the tiniest amount dropped onto a pillow to encourage sleep, or a single drop in an oil burner will scent your home and remind you of your time in Provence. A small array of items made from this precious oil are also for sale.

If the aromas aren't tempting enough to make you buy, then taste should convince you. Cheese can be sampled if you request it. This can be a necessity as often the ready prepared samples, placed conveniently for customers to help themselves are raided as soon as they appear, leaving nothing but the occasional crumb. If you're lucky enough to find a wine seller, then you'll be able to taste that too.

The local honey producer will let you sample their wares; a small teaspoonful to excite the taste buds and help you make the decision whether it's going to be a pot of mountain honey or the slightly sweeter lavender variety to take home with you. The honey is collected from hives placed in flower-filled mountain meadows, or on the edges of lavender fields and like Winnie the Pooh, I love honey, so never miss the opportunity to buy some and transport it back to the UK where I indulge in lacing my warming porridge with a spoonful on a cold and dark winter's morning.

The cured meats and sausages are also available to taste. The stall holder will offer you a small slice, often accompanied by a rapidly spoken and enthusiastic description explaining its origins and content. You can choose an olive from the olive stall to sample if you like; green, black, large or small, as long as you ask politely first, and if the olive oil stall has bagged a spot, you may be offered a small chunk of bread to dip into samples of the golden liquid.

Touch comes in handy, but it doesn't mean you can happily grope every bit of food you come across. You'd be very severely reprimanded if you did this. However, you're allowed to get 'hands-on' with some fruit and vegetables. No self-respecting local or French visitor will buy without first giving the item a thorough once over. Melons are squeezed to check for ripeness, along with tomatoes, peaches, avocados and anything else your average French shopper thinks appropriate.

As you continue to browse, there are so many sights and sounds to experience within our busy market. The bright colours of summer can be seen hanging from rails in the clothing stalls. One stall I can't resist sells the most beautiful silk dresses, trousers and tops. I never miss the opportunity to browse here, and on this occasion, I just had to buy the most beautiful dress in muted shades of purple and violet.

There is always a stall selling lovely examples of kitchenware, all made from olive wood, well-suited for such use as it is extremely hard with a very dense grain, as well as being resistant to odours and bacteria. The wood is shaped and polished to bring out the patterns that occur within the grain. They make the perfect presents, being decorative and useful.

We see the same stalls, in the same place, year after year during the summer months, but these are often joined by a hodgepodge of others selling anything from jewellery to mattresses, all fighting for attention within the melee. To add to this, throngs of tourists and locals stop to browse, buy or chat with neighbours. Dogs are brought along too, most of whom are curious to meet other canines, often much to the despair of their owners who are trying to buy cheese or some other delight while their enthusiastic dog is dragging on its lead in an attempt to get a good sniff of a passing four-legged stranger.

The market stalls thread themselves through the narrow streets of the old town, but as they emerge to populate the couple of small parking areas, visitors are obliged to park their cars in a nearby field, most of whom attempt to secure a place in a shady spot, with most unsuccessful and forced to return to an oven on wheels.

That particular morning we had arrived a little later, finding a cool spot under a tree, kindly left free by an early-bird marketgoer. We placed the dogs on their leads and headed towards a small wooden table, just outside the walls of the old town. Resting atop this table is a small scale, a metal cash box and several large wheels of my favourite cheese; the tasty, creamy Tomme de Montagne, produced locally with milk from cows that wander free in the lush green pastures of the mountains. I joined the back of a long queue which had snaked towards the road. I didn't hold out much hope of securing my chunk of cheese as this glorious stuff sells out in a heartbeat and as I edged closer to the front, very little was left of the huge wheels of Tomme with which the stallholder started his day. I was praying the lady in front wasn't about to buy all that was left. She didn't and I took the remaining piece plus a couple of the natural live yoghurts which he keeps in a tiny travel fridge resting on a small wall behind his table. The people standing behind me were not pleased to see me securing the final piece, but I'm sure they'd have done the same without a second thought.

We continued on, gathering provisions and stopping for a quick chat with another Olivier. He owns and runs the restaurant within one of the small squares inside the old town walls. As always, his tables, shaded by parasols, were brimming with lunchtime diners, so the chat proved to be quite brief as he rushed off to seat more clients and take their orders. We also bumped into Richard, who we'd not seen for quite a while. He was in fine fettle, happily settled with his new partner who we'd yet to meet, but as hospitable as ever, inviting us to knock on his door anytime and arrange for us to go for dinner one evening when we were next in residence.

With bags full of purchases, we made our way towards the little bar in the tiny Place Joseph Gireud. Tables were once again scattered under parasols and squeezed between the old buildings, one of which is the ancient Chapelle St Joseph and another, the tiny marie (town hall).

As always, it was packed with people, sheltering from the hot sun while nursing a cooling drink. They were also enjoying the music provided by two rather mature gentlemen, one armed with a guitar and the other with an accordion. It was great entertainment as the guitarist sang his way through the most diverse collection, including old French ditties, Rock n Roll Elvis, the Beatles 'Michell' and one obviously very popular Italian song with a chorus of 'ciao bella, ciao bella, ciao, ciao, ciao' which was heartily belted out by all, including Rob and me who can't speak Italian for toffee. There was something for everyone and the atmosphere was joyous, so much so, that several people rose to their feet and danced in the sunshine as music and laughter filled the air. We sat for a while soaking up the jovial atmosphere, chatting to an English gentleman we know, who we'd spied nursing a coffee. With a convenient stone water trough, fed by a constant stream of pure mountain water, the dogs didn't miss out either!

33

Out and About

Walk One – Le Bouchier

Our walking adventures continued as my itchy feet demanded movement and discovery. By mid to late afternoon, a bright morning would often transform into a dark maelstrom of lightning, thunder and sudden downpours. Summer in the mountains provides the perfect conditions due to the upward movement of warm air on their windward side, swooping up to the mountain tops, cooling as it reaches altitude, increasing humidity and forming storm clouds. With this in mind, we were always sure to head off out while the sun was still resting in a sea of blue sky. A couple of days earlier, I'd been browsing a specialist book of walking trails in the area and had noted a couple we'd not visited before. Time to set off and explore new territory.

Our first 'new' walk led to somewhere called Le Bouchier, lying within the shadow of Mont Pelat, the highest peak in our mountain chain at 3051 metres (10,000 feet) and alongside the small river which bears the village's name. I reassured Rob and the dogs that the walk didn't look too taxing and we could drive partway to join it.

The sunshine had become hazy by the time we arrived, but thankfully, any storm clouds were hovering elsewhere for the time being. Our walk commenced at the tiny chapel of St Peter which clung to the edge of a steep drop into a gorge, its front door a few feet from the edge. It then followed a route past a lone house, perched at the top of a steep slope, sitting amidst a field of flowers. It was a real joy and something of a shock to see such a riotous display of colour growing happily at such altitude and in such large numbers. I had no idea if I was trespassing, but I had to get close enough to take a photo or two of this extraordinary sight and left Rob on the footpath with the dogs as I struggled upslope to achieve this, carefully keeping watch to ensure I wouldn't find myself being shouted at by an angry householder.

Reaching a suitable spot, I noticed the area was surrounded by a fence made of plastic netting, within which lay a random display of tall, willowy blooms. Bright red poppies, yellow sunflowers, deep blue cornflowers and hollyhocks in shades of vivid pinks all added to this floral array. Not being a serious horticulturist I failed to recognise several other bright specimens nestling alongside. It really appeared whoever was responsible for this spectacle had simply tossed handfuls of seeds into the air, leaving the results to share their space with tall green weeds and grass. It was startlingly beautiful, the blooms nodding gently in the breeze creating a rippling technicolour sea set against a backdrop of dark mountains.

My photographer bones satisfied, I returned unseen to the safety of the footpath and a patient Rob. We continued on through the mountain scenery, high above the river Bouchier rushing by below us. Finally, after a short walk downhill, we reached the isolated community nestled within a green valley. We passed a grassy bank where some old wooden pews lay forlornly in disorganised rows, awaiting return to the dry interior of the small church of St Antoine, which according to the sign, had been erected in 1862. With no evidence of recent restoration work, it seemed they were in for a long wait before being rescued from the inclement weather. We continued along the rough track, muddy in parts due to summer storms passing through, noting the handful of mountain properties which appeared to form the entirety of this tiny place. We wandered further, seeing no sign of life except for one lady sitting on her balcony to whom we offered a *bonjour* as we passed by. The rough-hewn track continued on, leaving the village in its wake as it sought out a route delving deeper into the isolation of the high mountains. At this point, it seemed sensible not to venture further.

Time was inching towards late afternoon, so we retraced our steps back to the car, stopping briefly to chat with a French couple who had just alighted from their car and were intending to hike the pathway leading steeply towards the Col d'Allos, quite a distance away. We wished them a *bonne randonée,* loaded our weary dogs into the car and headed back, noting that the sun had become obscured behind a wall of dark ominous clouds and rumbles of distant thunder announced that an afternoon storm would soon be raging. By the time we arrived back at the house, it was as dark as night, with sheets of rain drowning roads and swelling the river Verdon. We watched from the windows as the lightning provided a continuous demonstration of the power of nature while the thunder roared above our heads.

Storms in the mountains can be extremely dangerous. These *tempêtes* often appear out of nowhere and quickly engulf unsuspecting hikers. Websites aimed at those who enjoy spending time in the mountains stress the importance of checking the local forecast before heading out. Once out, they recommend keeping a close eye on the weather around you, learning to recognise storm clouds and turning back immediately should any appear. Simply by being so high, the likelihood of a lightning strike becomes a real risk, along with rock falls, sudden floods, and exposure. The couple we met that day had been dressed for a casual hike but we did wonder why they began their lengthy trek when obviously a storm was highly likely, with dark clouds looming on the horizon. We very much hoped that common sense prevailed and they returned back to the safety of their car before venturing too far.

We both love our mountain storms when snuggled safely inside the house, as they're just so spectacular. Our view becomes immersed in a cauldron of dark clouds, bubbling up from behind the surrounding mountains and sweeping in our direction. It's not long before our entire valley disappears as the clouds penetrate deeper, finally surrounding our little house, bringing with them the rain and hail which batters our roof with a deafening roar. This is usually accompanied by a howling wind, driving the rain even harder. The lightning rips through the dark sky, plunging earthwards to ground itself on one of the mountain ridges, with the accompanying thunder creating an explosive bang before filling the air with a prolonged, rolling wave of sound, magnified as it rebounds from the walls of the surrounding peaks. There is no pause between light and sound as the storm takes no breath until it decides to head further along its path, taking its anger to rage elsewhere, finally dissipating when its fury is spent.

In the aftermath, our view gradually reveals itself once again, with puffs of cloud hovering within the trees as a nebulous sun appears, hiding behind a thin grey veil. Rain drips from the balcony and roof and distant rumbles remind us that the storm hasn't quite finished its torment yet. The river Verdon is turned from a gentle flow of crystal clear water into a turbulent ribbon of muddy opaqueness which will take a couple of days to disappear. Everything is sodden. The temperature starts to recover from shivering cold to warm and the birds suddenly find their voices once more. Often, the sun will decide to reveal itself in all its glory, the storm becoming a distant memory as the heat begins to erase all evidence of the deluge. At last, Rob and I can return to our outdoor chairs to catch the last rays before the sun hides itself behind the ridge. On such an evening following a storm, the sun will let us know it still has a final surprise in store, saying goodbye by producing the most dazzling sunsets. Splashed across the sky at the foot of the valley will be a swathe of burning colour, the pallet continually changing hue from deep purple to bright yellow as the sun slips lower and darkness falls.

Lac d'Allos

We'd spent the next couple of days staying close to home, shopping in town and trying to arrange to see Philippe for a beer. The poor man was working his socks off, his shop swamped from dawn 'til dusk with tourists topping up on their meaty necessities for lunch, dinner and BBQs. He'd employed an additional helper, a lady operating the till, leaving his two sons and a permanent employee to assist with service and prepping, but he was still exhausted at the end of a long day and his focus was on relaxing at home and sleep!

Gilbert and Annie were in residence for the whole of the month and had several visitors staying on and off throughout, but we still managed our usual chats, with Gilbert informing us that there had been new rules imposed for access to Lac d'Allos. Visitors have been permitted to drive as far as the car park before taking a forty minute uphill walk to reach the lake. In the summertime, as with all popular sites, it can get very busy with tourists wishing to see this phenomenon for themselves.

Lac d'Allos is Europe's highest natural glacial lake where swimming is strictly forbidden as the water is perilously cold and deep. This doesn't put visitors off as they come to walk around its perimeter, picnic alongside it or find a peaceful spot to simply sit and immerse themselves in nature. From a vantage point, in the right spot, it's possible to spy a marmot, the little creatures that occupy the mountainsides, digging their burrows to emerge in spring after hibernation to feed and explore. In summer, you can hear their calls as they warn others of encroaching danger, which may be an eagle soaring high above in the thermals or a human tramping past dragging a pushchair.

Most tourists to this area are responsible and respectful of nature, but there are always those who will lack any consideration for fellow visitors or their surroundings. We presumed that flora and fauna were suffering due to the amount of visitors during the finer weather and something needed to be done to keep numbers to manageable levels. Gilbert explained that from May through to the end of September, those wishing to park were required to book their place beforehand. It wasn't clear if limits were imposed on the amount of time permitted, or if the number of cars allowed had been reduced, but it was a good move to protect this wonderful spot where the quiet blue waters of the lake sit encircled by the mountain peaks within the stunning National Park.

Walk Two – Peyresc

My itchy footedness returned after a two-day respite. We'd not had any further storms and the weather had turned dry, sunny and warm.

"Shall we go for a walk today?" I asked Rob as I peered outside and noted the fine weather. "I've a great idea about where we can go."

My plan was to drive up to the Col de la St Michel, the location of a large cross-country ski area with marked trails, a restaurant/bar and several lodgings. The journey up is breathtaking as the initial route climbs rapidly, gaining around 356 metres (1167 feet) in a ridiculously short distance. The high road edges narrowly along the side of the mountain with a continuous run of precipitous sheer drops to the Verdon valley below. The views are spectacular, but the tiny concrete wall, there to prevent anyone from driving over the edge, does seem a tad inadequate! For the nervous, this part of the journey is relatively short before the route turns inland and continues to climb to the top where the land is level.

We packed the car with a picnic, loaded the dogs and were soon at our destination. We did a quick scan to ensure there were no sheep, cows or any other type of farm animals in the vicinity before releasing our happy hounds from their seat belts and out of the car. Our walk took us uphill, then uphill again, and again. Each time we thought we'd arrived at the top, another slope faced us. We were both sweaty and burning in the sun, so were over the moon when the trail entered woodland and some cool, comforting shade.

"Shit! Gerrof!" yelled Rob. I looked over to see what the problem was and observed him hopping about from foot to foot while whirling his arms above his head. Then stopping to slap an arm or leg.

"What on earth's the matter with you?" I questioned.

I received an "Ouch" in response, while he slapped his leg again. "It's these bloody biting flies! Hate the things. How come you're not being bitten?"

"I am occasionally, but they're not going to leave you alone if you continue to dance around like a demented witch doctor in lederhosen, wafting pheromones all over the place. As I see it, they're either attracted to you or see you as some large, hairy threat, but at least they're leaving me alone in the meantime, so keep going!"

"That's not very funny! I have a solution," and with that, he secured a small branch from a shrub just off the pathway and proceeded to swish it around his head to deter the creatures while I tried my best to ignore the things.

Eventually, we arrived at the top to find a large clearing containing a telephone mast and a very strange, stone-built something or other. We had no idea what it was. It was four-sided and resembled a weeny house suitable for hobbits. It narrowed a little towards the top and had a chimney-shaped object jutting from the flat roof. It had no doors or windows so any hobbit habitation was impossible and besides, it appeared solid. We scratched our heads wondering what it could be and decided it was simply the result of some silly individual's desire to create a folly to confuse visitors like us.

The dogs were happy exploring the greenery and I was happy, but frustrated, pursuing the most beautiful, supersized butterfly who continued to have the last laugh by dropping soundlessly onto a clump of tiny flowers, teasing me into a suitable crouching position to practise my wildlife photography, then taking off before the shutter on my camera had time to click. In the meantime, Rob, perched uncomfortably on a rock, was becoming increasingly impatient, waving his branch furiously as the flies continued their bombardment. Failing miserably at butterfly photography, I made my fly-pestered husband's day by suggesting we return to the car.

We took an alternative and much shorter route down and to Rob's relief, were soon fly free, the nasty sods happily munching on walkers elsewhere. Our picnic was consumed quickly, eating it out of the back of the car, the dogs receiving their fair share of our food and water. It was time to move on and visit somewhere we'd been dying to explore.

We were heading further along the road, taking a left turn to the village of Peyresc. We'd been told many years ago, that this isolated place originated from the eleventh century but had, in recent times, become a Belgian enclave. We were really curious to see if it was housing some strange Flemish cult and set off to find out. The journey along this quiet road was simply wonderful, with far-reaching views over forested valleys which descended towards Annot and beyond. At one point, a couple of the village houses could be seen across the void, teetering on the edge of a precipice. Eventually, the road snaked around a bend squeezing between a narrow gap cut through the natural stone and continued past a wall of fascinating rock formations. This was literally the end of the road.

We parked the car in a safe spot, put the dogs on their leads and left to admire the view. I was in my element, running back the way we'd come to take photos of the rock formations and to explore the top of a promontory containing a strange collection of stone carvings, one of which was a large lump of free-standing rock, carved out to form a covered seat. On closer inspection, this curious collection, scattered about on the level grassy terrain, determined their origins must have been an old chapel, no longer standing, though a large cross had been erected to mark the spot. Having spent an age in the company of my phone camera, I indicated with some manic gesticulations aimed at the Rob-shaped speck in the distance that I was on my way back to rejoin him and the dogs.

We headed into a narrow street between some ancient houses, reaching a small square containing a little chapel. Further explorations through the tiny alleyways led us to some stone steps leading upwards then spiralling higher to disappear behind more old properties. At the foot of the steps, we encountered a friendly Frenchman who told us he resided in a village not far from our own. We stopped to chat as he was interested in us and our dogs and we were curious to find out more about the place.

He couldn't offer a detailed history but told us the village was indeed Belgian and an academic enclave where students from several Belgian universities would be accommodated on field trips. It was a beautiful environment in which to study, able to venture out into the extraordinary surroundings to observe nature and extend knowledge in such subjects as ecology, botany, zoology, geography and geology. Not just the sciences either as it would be an ideal venue for artists.

It seemed he and his wife were just packing up to leave for home and it became evident they were employed to keep the student population happy. A clothesline full of washed bedding drying in the sunshine and the fact his wife was finalising the washing up in what looked like a refectory, gave us a clue as to their probable roles of cook, housekeeper and caretaker.

As always, my curiosity was getting the better of me and I needed to find out more. The village has indeed a long history, but I wanted to focus on more recent times, wondering how Peyresc had been rescued, restored and turned into such a specialist destination. As with many isolated villages, it had been slowly abandoned as people moved to find a living elsewhere, leaving their homes to dereliction; the weight of snow causing roofs to cave in, the walls to slowly crumble and nature to steadily encroach and take hold.

The village's saviour arrived in the shape of a gentleman named Georges Lambeau, who in 1952 stumbled across this collection of ruins. He and his Belgian friend formed the idea of setting up a humanist centre for students, teachers and artists to be brought together for research and discussion. An accidental meeting with a young architect pushed the dream of rebuilding the village forward, remaining faithful to the Provençal style of architecture and use of materials. With the help of many, including thousands of Belgian student builders, employed over a thirty year period, the dream was finally realised.

Such was its success that the village was awarded the *Chefs-d'oeuvre en Péril* (Endangered Masterpieces) prize in 1980, awarded by President Giscard d'Estaing in person.

Walk Three - An Unexpected Lunch

Our final trek was a familiar route along a gravel road that led to the bottom of a ski lift at Seignus. We knew there would be no new discoveries, but were surprised to find the small ski snack bar open. It's a tiny place with all its seating outside to allow hungry skiers a break from the slopes, but we'd never seen it open in summertime. Two of the chair lifts remain operational in July and August to carry mountain bikes and their riders up to the top of specialist trails, presenting them with varied, steep terrain and impossible obstacles. It's a recognised competition trail for VTT (*Velo Tout Terrain*) and extremely challenging. We've watched several cyclists haring down at speed, standing on their pedals, leaning back to prevent being thrown over the handlebars, swerving around bends, flying off bumps, leaping over gaps and somehow managing to avoid hitting a tree. We think they're totally bonkers, but then people think Rob and I are totally bonkers for sliding down mountains on skis. Each to their own!

Hikers and casual walkers also use the lifts to gain access to the myriad of footpaths that stretch for miles and others choose to simply bring a picnic and enjoy the tranquillity. We've used the lifts in summer several times and were allowed to take the dog too. Our previous little Fox Terrier, Maxwell, was perfectly used to it, lying quietly across us while Rob hung tightly onto his safety harness. Those days are now gone as dogs are no longer permitted, so if we want to head for the heights accompanied by the dogs, we have to walk up!

Seeing this little place open, it seemed rude not to stop for a cold beer. Fifteen minutes later, we were tucking into a huge cheese omelette each, served with hot crispy fries. We couldn't resist after the aroma of cooking made us feel hungry, not helped by seeing other diners tucking into appetising plates of food. The dogs were successful in scrounging fries and the serving lady kindly delivered a bowl of fresh water to help quench their thirst after the long walk up.

Our descent back down was easy enough but while we'd been guzzling our food, storm clouds had begun to gather over some distant peaks and faint rumbles of thunder announced the need to get back to the car before the storm hit. The sun disappeared and the sky became grey, but the storm remained at a distance and eventually had a change of mind, altering course to become a menace elsewhere.

34

Off to Lac Leman via the Route des Grandes Alpes

Our time at the house had come to an end but our holiday continued with a five-day stay on a campsite on the banks of Lac Leman (many refer to it as Lake Geneva). I was reuniting with my long-time friend Cynthia whom I'd met aged sixteen at college and who married and moved to Lausanne aged nineteen. We'd seen one another on and off across the years but much of her life had been incredibly difficult. I am so grateful that she is finally free from the cruelties she suffered at the hands of her husband and his family—a story waiting to be told.

We were staying on the French side of the lake, in Thonon les Bains and we decided to reach our destination by travelling along the Route des Grandes Alpes, rather than suffer the *autoroute*. Car once more packed to the gunnels, we set off, sad to be leaving, but looking forward to our next adventure.

Our journey took us over the Col to Barcelonette and then tracked the Ubaye River to Lac Serre Ponçon. This enormous reservoir's claim to fame is that it is the largest manmade lake in France, fed by the Ubaye and Durance rivers, with one of the largest earthen hydroelectric dams in Europe. It's quite something to behold at 123 metres high (400+ feet), 600 metres wide (1,968 feet) and 650 metres thick (over 2,000 feet)! I can remember visiting it years ago and walking along the top. The lake is a beautiful sight with its turquoise blue waters, especially when you see it from the viewpoint along the road to Digne les Bains. However, my carefully plotted route took us in a different direction, along the high road on the lake's eastern side, heading north.

We progressed towards the Vallée de la Guisane, in ski country, the clue being the ski lifts we could see which served the popular and well-known resort of Serre Chevalier. Skiing was the last thing on our minds on such a hot, sunny day and our attention was definitely focused on eating. Stomachs were rumbling, so when we spied a large car park just off the road in Salle les Alpes, we decided to park and hunt for food. With the dogs safely on their leads, we crossed a small bridge and found ourselves in a little street decorated with bunting, flapping about in the breeze. We presumed the *Tour de France* had passed by judging from the images of the *Tour's* famous race shirts displayed on the tiny flags.

A restaurant had set up a shaded terraced area across the road from its premises, right next to a small alpine river which we could hear gushing towards heaven knows where. The heat was oppressive, so being offered a table under the large awning to enjoy a light lunch was truly welcome. After treats, water and a walk, the dogs were content to settle back into the car for the next stage of the journey, though Teddy was disappointed after failing to drag us into the river.

I'd planned our journey to purposely include one of the highest mountain passes in Europe. In my trusty map book, it is shown as very wiggly route resembling a string of sausages concertinaed together as it heads north from the Col de Lauteret up to the Col du Galibrier and beyond. It's also pretty steep in parts, the road achieving a scary 13.1% gradient. As the *Tour de France* often chooses this death-defying, stomach-churning long climb upwards (then downwards), it's incredibly popular with amateur cyclists who for some reason, have the compunction to try it themselves. Motorbikers also love to attack it because of the plentiful hairpin bends, forcing their bikes over as they speed around them, almost scraping off their kneecaps in the process while, somehow, managing to avoid the cyclists who are pedalling like fury. I've never been so happy to be in a vehicle with four wheels, powered steering and servo-assisted brakes. Having said that, we knew what we were in for, having travelled this way before, twice, once northbound and once southbound and we love it.

Just below the highest point, we pulled in at a popular spot, which on that day was packed with people heading to the restaurant and gift shop. Leaving the hungry and souvenir starved to their amusements, I wandered up a footpath which led me to a prime vantage point atop a grassy knoll. Opposite, loomed the majestic peaks of the Massif des Ecrins. It's a huge area covering nearly one thousand square kilometres (386 square miles), with the highest peak, Barre des Ecrins, reaching 4,102 metres (13,458 feet). The area is also stuffed with glaciers, comprising a total of forty if only counting the main ones, plus a host of smaller secondaries.

I had no idea which of the glaciers were on show before me, but having stood in this same spot, armed with my camera fifteen years ago, I was shocked and saddened to see how much these magnificent rivers of ice had retreated. One small glacier had disappeared completely, the only sign of its existence being a gully of grey shale meandering down to join the road. The mightiest in the region, the Glacier Blanc, was nearly six kilometres long in 2002 but regular monitoring has shown that after the lowest winter snowfall for twenty-three years and the largest summer melt, this leviathan lost four times more mass in 2022 than the combined yearly averages since 2002. I stood for a while, wondering how long these giants of the natural world would survive before they are lost forever.

I was snapped out of my reverie as Rob approached. He'd been taking the dogs for a leg stretch and wee and reminded me we really needed to get moving if I wanted to stop at the Col and then make it to our campsite, still a long distance away, before darkness. We arrived at the summit safely to find a crush of bicycles, motorbikes, cars and camper vans all vying to park. Folk were posing for photos in front of the altitude sign or struggling to get everything in on a selfie. It was sheer madness.

We luckily managed to squeeze ourselves into a proper parking space before heading to the outlook. I'll leave you to imagine the view, populated as it is with some of the highest peaks in the French Alps.

Several hours later, still a few kilometres from our destination, I rang our campsite to let them know we might be late and was told reception closed at 7.00 pm The guy on the other end of the phone asked for our current location. Having fortuitously just driven past a signpost we were able to supply accurate information. He explained we'd be OK and would make it in good time. We didn't! He hadn't anticipated the stupidity of us getting lost no more than ten minutes away from it, or attempting to gain entry into a campsite we'd not booked. We left that one shamefaced after banging on the main gates to be let in, shouting to those milling about inside to find the receptionist. She finally arrived, examined our booking document and directed us to our booked site further along the same road. It was now 7.25 pm and we finally arrived in a bit of panic, wondering if we could sneak into the site and check in the next morning. The gods were obviously smiling upon us as the reception was open, so our nice chap on the end of the phone earlier had given us duff information. It closed at 7.30 pm and we'd made it just in time.

Camping, Exploring and a Reunion

Finally, on our pitch, we were aware everyone around us was eating dinner seated on their chalet balconies or outside their camper vans, no doubt happy we'd arrived to provide the evening's entertainment. Our audience appeared enthralled by two pensioners erecting a massive tent in the fading light, managing to get the thing up without injury or making a complete cobbler's of it. It was dark by the time we'd finished, our audience had lost interest earlier as nothing remotely amusing had occurred. Our late night ended after a quick shower, a rush to the bar for a well-deserved couple of beers and then collapsing alongside our dogs to sleep well before being rudely awakened early the next morning by some yapping mutt next door, accompanied by loud shushing as the owner tried to shut it up.

The lake was a mere ten minutes from our pitch, across a park where people could sit on a bench, lounge on the grass in the sunshine or, if suffering the intense heat of the sun, choose to shelter under the shady canopy provided by one of the mature trees. The beach was just below a grassy slope where steps had kindly been provided to protect unsteady individuals from the embarrassment of an undignified bottom slide to reach it.

Calling it a beach was a bit of an overstatement to be honest. It was devoid of any beachy accoutrements due to the lack of space, forcing people to sit on their towels, though trees growing on the bank behind did make up for the lack of parasols. To distract the mind away from these minor discomforts your main focus is the panorama before you. The huge expanse of blue water stretches into the far distance and through the haze it's possible to see Switzerland on the opposite bank. Tall mountains surround much of the lake, their higher altitudes still clutching onto outcrops of winter snow. Yachts and small boats bob about in the distance and closer to shore, a paddle boarder might slowly drift past or a small group of canoers out for a leisurely paddle.

Covering 582 square kilometres (nearly 225 square miles) it's easy to appreciate this is the world's largest alpine lake. Split between France and Switzerland, it was formed by the Rhone glacier back in the ice age, along with lakes Annecy and Bourget to the south. It really is a beautiful spot, with Geneva on its western shore and some picturesque and interesting small towns and villages around the perimeter such as Evian les Bains in France, famous for its waters and Montreux in Switzerland, famous for its jazz festival and a favourite home of Freddy Mercury, where you will find a wonderful bronze statue of him in full performance stance, positioned at the water's edge.

I'm a bit of a water baby, so persuaded Rob to spend an afternoon at our beach, allowing myself the pleasure of a swim in the warm and surprisingly clear water. Teddy and Maisie decided to join in, doggie paddling frantically to reach me as I swam lazily about just offshore. Teddy was in his element and easily made it, but poor little Maisie, who only swims to show Teddy she can, arrived to say a quick hello before immediately turning back to shore. With her little legs going flat out and not making much progress, I was forced to assist, clutching her harness, keeping her safe until her paws made contact with terra firma, whereupon she ran to Rob to shake enthusiastically, before heading to the water's edge to bark, her way of making us give in to her demands and join her. Teddy took no notice, happily doing his thing until Rob decided to throw sticks into the water to keep our dogs amused. Until this point, I'd been happily floating on my back, absorbed in my own little world when reality intruded in the shape of a frantic Teddy trying to grab a stick that had just sought me out as the target. Maisie then started barking again, disturbing the peace. Rob had a huge grin on his face as I emerged, dragging a growling Teddy onto the beach, his jaws locked tight onto the stick I was now holding.

"Were you aiming at me on purpose?"

"No." said Rob, still grinning. "I was just throwing the stick a little further as you know how much Teddy likes to swim. It was purely accidental. Honest."

Of course, he was lying, his innocent expression fooling no one, but he was forgiven as I'd have probably done the same to him! All watery escapades now at an end and the sun telling us it was late afternoon, our soggy four-legged companions were placed on their leads and we headed back.

A Day Out to Châtel

Leaving Lac Leman behind the following day, we stretched our explorations further by taking a day's trip to Châtel. It was a beautiful drive along forested roads, alongside rivers and streams and passing through tiny hamlets. We decided to pull over and stop at the village of Abondance, famous for producing cheese of the same name, making sure we purchased a slab to enjoy back at the tent. I wasn't in charge of the cheese buying and took my eye off the ball as Rob agreed to the amount the lady server had indicated with her very large cheese knife. The slab was huge and presented us with enough to feed half the campsite. Even my credit card cringed when it came to paying for it.

Rob swore he hadn't realised how big a chunk it was until it had been cut away and was then too embarrassed to ask for less. I didn't believe him for one minute.

We lingered long enough to explore the pretty village and pop into a little bakery to buy lunch, finding deserted seating outside a closed bar to sit awhile in the sunshine and chomp through our cheese and ham baguettes. Back on the road, it was onwards and upwards, finally reaching our destination and parking near a very small lake, attracting our attention, as at its centre was an impressive mini version of Geneva's famous *Jet d'Eau*, the 140 metre (459 feet) plume of water situated in Geneva's harbour. The dogs enjoyed a walk around the lake, Teddy managed a short swim and later they both experienced their first trip in a *télécabine*, transporting us up to the heights of the ski resort. A lengthy stroll followed as we explored the summit and marvelled at the panorama, finding we'd crossed the border into Switzerland, the only marker to show we were in a different country being a Swiss flag flying at the top of a tall flag pole.

Hello and Goodbyes

It was finally the day when Cynthia was arriving on the ferry from Lausanne. The weather was looking grey, but our reunion was nothing but sunshine. I'd not seen my friend face to face for four years and we had a lot of catching up to do. Along with Rob and the dogs, we enjoyed the best of days, ending too soon as Cynthia had to catch the return ferry, leaving early evening. Delivering her to the port, Rob left me to accompany my friend to the dockside to say our goodbyes, making promises to see each other again soon. The weather had deteriorated with light rain and storm clouds hovering on the horizon. I hoped Cynthia wouldn't be subjected to a vomit-inducing boat trip across the lake, as it's famous for churning up two-metre waves in stormy conditions. She text later to say all was well.

The storm eventually arrived just as we were snuggling into our sleeping bags, keeping us awake as torrential rain threatened to drill through the roof while the wind was busy shaking the walls. It was virgin territory for our tent, and I didn't help Rob's attempt to sleep by continually asking him:

"Are you sure it's properly waterproof? It won't blow away will it? It's howling out there."

"For God's sake Jane, it won't leak and it won't blow away, it's made to cope with these conditions. We're safely battened down. You saw me checking the tent pegs and tightening everything. Just go to sleep and quit worrying!"

Thankfully he was right and we awoke to a glorious morning, our tent still standing, but the roof festooned with soggy leaves, the guilty party being a nearby tree that failed to hang onto much of its canopy during the storm.

Our days by Lac Leman passed by too quickly. Departure day was soon upon us and it was time to pack away our temporary home. We tackled the self-inflating mattress first, wrestling the damn thing to roll it into a suitable size for its bag. After four attempts we failed miserably, tied it up with string and dumped it in the car, eyeing it with hatred as after a hard, sweaty fight to contain it, the perishing thing now occupied twice the amount of space it should have. The final task was the tent itself, the exterior having been swept clean of leaves and ants. With it lying crumpled and deflated at our feet, we scratched our heads having forgotten how we unfolded it, the point of which was to repeat this manoeuvre in reverse. Obviously, we'd suffered a joint senior moment and couldn't remember, but after the odd mistake, we issued a small cheer as it slid nicely into the bag. The dogs, tied to a tree, watched on quietly, obviously discussing amongst themselves why these two humans with a combined age of 952 in dog years, even attempted this camping malarkey.

PART VI

AUTUMN ADVENTURES

35

Strikes, Friends and Geology

'Season of mists and mellow fruitfulness,
Close bosom-friend of the maturing sun.'
— *John Keats*

A wistful reminder of autumn from John Keats, but the start of our annual autumn trip certainly lacked the romanticism of his famous poem which should have read *'Season of twits and bloody mindedness'* as certain French citizens decided to demonstrate this trait by striking, closing six oil refineries and reducing fuel deliveries by 60%. This meant forecourts had to close once their supply of diesel and petrol ran out. It left Rob and me in a bit of a quandary. Should we stay at home or should we risk it? Not ones to give in, we headed to the Tunnel after borrowing an old, metal, army-type jerry can from a mate, then filling it to the brim with diesel. We checked this type of container was permissible when travelling through the Tunnel and placed it within easy reach in case customs deemed we looked suspicious and conducted a search for drugs. We were a little miffed when they didn't bother as we missed demonstrating how very clever and sensible we'd been in transporting our own fuel to get us out of any expensive difficulties.

The Tunnel was the quietest we'd ever seen it. The dread of

running out of fuel, with only a random handful of fuel stations open, had obviously deterred many people from hopping across the channel. The site was deserted, with the amount of people milling around amounting to a dozen or so, most of whom would have been employees. The train departed carrying just three cars.

We spent our first night in St Omer but had arranged to meet up with our friends, Bob and Sylviane, at a delightful hotel we'd booked the following night near Lyon. It being not too distant from their home, we'd invited them to join us for a meal in the restaurant. In the past we'd often stayed with them at their home, but this hadn't happened for a while as Bob had been ill. It was our treat as they'd always been so hospitable towards us, feeding us aperitifs and utterly delicious four-course dinners. It was our opportunity to pay them back for their friendship and kindness. All we had to do was to get there safely without any mishaps.

"What's that noise?" I said as we were heading down the *autoroute* just past Reims.

"What noise?" questioned Rob.

"Something is wrong. Can't you hear it? It's a rattling noise. Please don't tell me the car is about to throw another wobbly!"

"It can't be anything serious as the car was checked thoroughly at the garage before we came away. I can hear it, but it doesn't sound serious."

"You said that the last time and look what happened. You need to pull over to see what it is before something important drops off."

Pulling over onto the hard shoulder, Rob got out, did that thing of kicking the tyres, shaking the wheels and looking around the car. He was back in the driving seat rather quickly.

"So? What is it then?"

"Nothing to worry about. Seems there's a bit of a loose panel by the wheel arch. I've pushed it back into place and it should be okay."

Ten minutes later.

"That noise is back!"

"Yeah, I know," said Rob.

"So do something!"

"Stop panicking. Just about everything that can drop off this car has been replaced or repaired. It's a tough motor and it'll keep going for years!"

"Yeah, right. Well, you'd better stop in one of the rest areas and have a good look around this tough motor to see what that rattling is before we're left stranded … again!"

We pulled off and we both proceeded to examine every square inch. I left Rob to do the underneath as I wouldn't have a clue what to look for anyway. The dogs were going crazy as they wanted to get out for a toilet break, so I obliged and granted their wish, leaving Rob to his motor vehicle sleuthing. I arrived back after ten minutes to find Rob looking smug.

"Found it! You'll never guess what it is."

"So, have I got to guess or are you going to tell me."

"It's that."

He was pointing to the back of the roof where that funny antenna thing sits. I climbed on the back bumper allowing me to examine it more closely. It had come unstuck and was clinging on by its wiry arms which still seemed attached to something. We discussed what to do. Leaving it might mean the thing could fly off and be the cause of a major pile-up. We couldn't pull it out as it had multiple wires going heaven knows where and we didn't want to risk completely knackering the electrics. The decision was made to find something to secure it. Door pockets, rear storage areas and seat pockets were all searched to no avail. Then I had a light bulb moment and opened the glove box to find a small tube of super glue I'd remembered seeing, bought to glue down something else in the car no doubt. The glue was applied liberally to seal the rubber underside of the antenna to the roof and we waited until it felt secure and safe enough to continue our journey. I thoroughly recommend super glue as the thing stayed put for weeks until Rob took it to a garage to get it properly looked at.

Although slightly fraught about the fuel situation, it seemed that there were more garages open than anticipated. After all these years of heading back and forth, we know where to find cheaper fuel, preventing the need to buy the stuff at exorbitant prices on the *autoroute*. All our usual places were open and serving diesel, though we did pass many showing *ferme* (closed) or *pas de gazole* (no diesel).

Before leaving the UK, I usually get a request email from Bob, listing foodstuffs he can't locate easily in France. In the past, we've taken bacon and Cumberland sausages, mince pies, custard powder and Christmas puddings to name a few. Post-Brexit rules mean we can no longer take a host of fresh produce, but one of the permissible things Bob wanted this time was tea. The French are great with food, wine and coffee, but tea? No. Their popular brand is a little too insipid for our British tastes and what he needed was some good old 'builders' tea', made for a mug and not a delicate china cup.

After dinner and saying goodbye to our lovely friends, we held a bit of a swap shop in the car park, with food items being passed between us. Bob was pleased with his tea bags and we really appreciated our favourite onion tart that Sylviane always makes for us, plus a bagful of walnuts from their tree. I think we got the best of the bargain for sure! We waved them off but not before we'd received an invitation to stay when back over for our next break in February.

The Geopark

The weather at the house turned out to be fabulously unseasonal, with summer-like temperatures and days filled with bright sunshine. We'd each packed two tee shirts 'just in case' which were now earning their keep, while jumpers were idling in the wardrobe. Now was the time to tackle the upstairs window shutters, with eight scruffy and worn examples in need of some love and care. The endless sunshine offered the perfect conditions to finally get this job placed on the 'done' list.

We'd brought along a sander so we didn't have to beg Gilbert for his, and dug out the large tin of varnish from the tool cupboard. I checked to see it hadn't set into a viscous lump and considered whether the amount left in the tin was adequate to do the job. There was no way I wanted to run out half-way through.

A trip down to the large DIY store was planned to buy another tin and some weed killer. I don't like using it, but our pristine pebbled area had taken on the appearance of a wheat field. I couldn't face trying to manually remove all of it, spending hours on my hands and knees knowing if I didn't get the grass roots out, the annoying greenery would be back to haunt me again on our next visit.

We set off mid-morning on yet another glorious day, heading for the *Centre de Commerce* on the outskirts of Digne les Bains, managing to leave the DIY store with only the two items we wanted, having been tempted by lots of other lovely stuff, but resisting for once. We then headed to the huge hypermarket to stock up on foodie essentials, treats and to see if they'd any fuel at their pumps. They had plenty, so with our tank filled it was a short hop back to the town centre and our next stop; a late lunch at a popular restaurant we know, where we joined many others eating outside in the sunshine. While enjoying our lunch of fish and chips – yes the French do them too – and a small carafe of rosé wine, I suggested we make our way back to the house via the back route, taking us over the Col de Corobin.

With the sun still shining we commenced our return journey through a steep sided valley, passing the thermal baths, enjoying the quiet scenic route which gradually gained height until the Col is reached at 1230 metres (just over 4,000 feet). We stopped to stretch all twelve legs, pausing to take in the autumnal view. It was quite extraordinary. In the forefront were the sweeping, sloping curves of what is called 'black earth', though it is actually Black Marl or Marlstone, formed under the sea in the Jurassic period. These dune-like stony outcrops, called *robines*, are more suited to a lunar landscape and look incredibly incongruous amidst the lush landscapes in which they exist. We'd often come across these unusual vistas when out and about and initially believed them to be remnants of lava flows, but with no ancient volcanos within hundreds of miles, we were very wide of the mark. Admittedly they look quite bleak as their mineral composition doesn't sustain much vegetation, except for a few thorny shrubs. However, it being autumn, these thorny shrubs were putting on a bit of a show in their flame-bright colours which positively glowed against their dark backdrop.

When we purchased our little home, we had no idea that it sat in a world-renowned geological area. We found out that 568,300 acres (nearly 230,000 hectares) of our Haut Provence was the first reserve of its kind to receive the UNESCO Geopark label, back in 2000. Dignes les Bains holds its headquarters and nearby is the famous *Dalle aux Ammonites,* a huge slab of rock containing more than 1500 ammonites, some as big as seventy centimetres in diameter. We've not seen this yet, but have searched for fossils near St Andre and along with friends, walked to the *Valleé des Siréniens,* near Castellane, to view the cliff wall containing a series of manatee skeletons. It was quite a sight, even if geological interests aren't top of your list.

36

At Les Hirondelles

Gilbert was in residence for a few days. Although living in Cannes with the Mediterranean at his feet, he prefers the mountains, spending as much time as possible several thousand feet above it. He often comes up for a couple of days and then has to return because he has a scheduled event to attend, such as his regular English classes.

Chatting one day, we asked if Annie was going to join him before he headed back. He answered in the negative and explained she'd recently had a stent fitted in her heart. Thankfully, Gilbert reassured us she was fine and back on her feet after being discharged a couple of weeks earlier. When Gilbert mentioned she was now eighty-two years old, it came as quite a shock. For some reason, we've never considered Annie to be in her eighties. She certainly doesn't look it and certainly doesn't lack energy. She is also still in possession of a sharp mind. As you already know, Gilbert is as fit as a butcher's dog and it seems residents around our town live to a ripe old age, still going strong well into their nineties. It's not exactly Shangri La, but I'm sure our mountain air consists of some strange life-extending elixir. I just hope it works for Rob and me!

The next day dawned sunny once again, so with my work area set up outside the door, it was time for some elbow grease and a big push to finish the remaining shutters. I was happily varnishing, using what was left in the old tin, knowing the sun would dry them in a jiffy and I'd be able to complete it all in a couple of days. How wrong I was. For the first time since arriving the previous week, obviously waiting until I was about to start work, shower clouds had snuck in and it started to rain. I was in and out of the house like a figure on a cuckoo clock, placing shutters, still sticky with varnish, close to the wall in the partial shelter provided by the eaves of the house. Once the sun broke through the clouds, I'd rush out again to spend half an hour or so before the next fall of rain stopped work. This continued for five days and was slowly driving me bonkers. Finally, with the job completed, Rob fitted the last shutter at the window. If I had a trumpet, I'd have played a fanfare! The new tin of medium oak we'd bought remained unopened and the aroma of white spirit and varnish no longer hung around me like a cloud. I could now begin to nag Rob as to why he hadn't succeeded in fixing our 'new' TV, which for some reason decided to lose the signal a few days before our departure back to the UK.

This loss of signal was frustrating and annoying. Once our temperature dropped as the sun disappeared to warm the southern hemisphere, it was often pleasant to curl up in front of the fire and choose to watch a bit of Auntie Beeb (BBC) or similar. Before it all went caput, we'd settle down to catch up with the news, but this seemed to go from bad to worse, with the UK's political situation playing out like a scene from *Spitting Image*. I'm sure the makers of this iconic old TV show would have taken huge delight in depicting the unfortunate Ms Truss and her economic shenanigans. With war in the Ukraine sadly raging still and doom and gloom at every turn, we eventually avoided it altogether before our 'mental 'elf' started to suffer, choosing to watch something a bit more cheerful instead. Our TV was feeling miserable, so it also gave up on the news but went too far when it blanked all other TV channels. Rob was asked to provide the magic and fix it.

He tried, he really did, but all was lost. We did find out it wasn't our new TV, so apologised profusely while hurling abuse at the satellite dish instead. We even pondered the possibility of some idiot tech person incorrectly pushing a button that sent the transmitting satellite hurling into outer space. The truth was, we hadn't a clue and decided to leave it until our next visit when Rob could spend more time struggling.

Talking of signals, one good thing was my new mobile phone. I was in love with it. I could see the screen clearly for starters, it also responded immediately when I moved the icons around or selected a menu and best of all, it had a brilliant camera with built-in editing software. The man in our UK phone shop was shocked I was still using my old one, reminding me mobiles weren't designed to last quite that long!

Rob and I also found that phone signals had suddenly improved, texts flew, emails arrived or departed without delay, phone calls didn't result in robotic speech or interrupted conversations and my Facebook posts, with a few attached photos, would actually send, well most of the time. The reason for this fortuitous turn of events was a second communications mast I spied, peeking up between pines on the mountain slope not far from its friend. We were delighted but still lived in hope that Philippe's rumours of cable laying would one day be a certainty.

Philippe, Michel and Olivier the restaurateur

We hadn't seen Philippe as he was away enjoying a break, leaving his sons in control of the shop. At this time of year, the queues have long gone and the shop happily receives a more manageable flow of customers. Waiting in the shop one morning, I realised that Michel was standing in front of us chatting away to a local. Michel was the previous owner of Les Hirondelles who had bought a much larger residence a little further up the mountainside from us. He was about to walk out of the shop when I called his name. He was rather surprised to see us standing there, but recognised us at once. We held a brief conversation, asking after Sylvanna, his wife. He told us she was very unwell, but didn't go into detail, wished us *bon vacances* and rushed off. This behaviour was really unusual as he's normally an outgoing, friendly person and we suspected he needed to get away before we enquired further. We sincerely hoped that whatever Sylvanna was suffering from wasn't serious as she's always been a jovial soul, funny and full of life.

It was approaching lunchtime, and a brief stop for a quick coffee outside Olivier's restaurant was considered necessary, especially as we caught that aroma of fresh coffee in the air as we passed by. Now approaching the end of his seasonal opening, Olivier had time to pause for a proper chat rather than the brief *"Salut, ça va?"* as he rushes about taking orders. We knew he would be closing his restaurant in a couple of days as trade slowly reduces from the end of September through to the end of October. It's the time when many local business people, who have worked non-stop through the summer months, take the opportunity for a well-deserved holiday.

Olivier was heading to Ireland almost as soon as his restaurant door swung shut for the final time. We discovered he is a huge fan of the country and especially loves the food served in restaurants along the west coast, telling us the fish and seafood were the best he'd ever eaten. We explained we were quite familiar with the Emerald Isle having travelled to the north and south as Rob has Irish genes, inherited from his grandad born in County Kildare. We talked for a while about the country's merits – its people, the food, Guinness and whisky—and its downfall—the rain. Before we left, he asked for Rob's mobile number and gave us his, explaining he was working in the ski resort of Pra Loup over the winter period and if we could make it over, to give him a ring. After a handshake for Rob, kissed cheeks for me and a *très bon vacances* for Olivier, we took our leave and headed back home.

37

Dog Troubles

Dog Troubles – Maisie's Story

Life with two dogs is never simple, but I admit our two haven't given us much trouble. Both are now into their senior years with Teddy just over two years older than Maisie, but both are healthy, happy and have never been the cause of worry while in France, until now. Let's start with Maisie's story.

I know I've told you about our vet and his casual attitude with regard to treating animals and working out his fees, but he really did a grand job when it came to little Maisie.

We'd noticed that she was rather lethargic, happy to sleep rather than play or go for walks. She then began to yelp when she moved. She was subjected to much poking and prodding from Rob and me to find where and what the issue might be. We then scoured her coat for signs of cuts, foreign bodies or tics. She didn't make a murmur throughout either process and we'd found nothing untoward. It was such an intermittent thing that we considered she might have had a bit of a knock when playing or exploring outside and was suffering mild consequences. She could still walk and was eating and drinking, so we left her for a couple of days. Once again, on occasion, she'd issue a tiny yelp when rising to her feet, so it was time to take her to see Mr Vet.

Rob took on the responsibility of taking her. Teddy went along too, not for any kind of canine paw holding for Maisie's benefit, but we required the doggie passport necessities, saving another trip down a couple of days later. Rob was issued with strict instructions to call as soon as he was out of the surgery. I stayed at the house to continue with the vanishing job, which helped a little to remove my thoughts from what might be wrong with our little girl.

When Rob finally emerged from the vet's office, he rang to say Mr Vet had given Maisie the most thorough examination he'd ever seen. Her legs were individually rotated and stretched, each vertebrae was pressed, her stomach manipulated, her paws, ears and eyes examined and her teeth checked. Then her head was swivelled side to side, her heart listened to, her temperature taken and an undignified examination of the internal workings of her anus was conducted! Throughout the whole process, Maisie was calm and remained silent. Rob said he was hoping she'd emit at least one little squeak to prove he wasn't lying, but nothing. Rob was speechless and Mr Vet gave one of those gallic shrugs, admitting there was nothing he could find wrong and judged her to be fit and healthy. After receiving a pain-killing injection just in case, she was removed from the examination table, wagging her tail. Rob was issued with tablets for her to take over the next couple of days and Mr Vet did his usual guesswork of pulling a price out of thin air. Our fraud of a dog instantly returned to her old self and we've never heard that yelp again.

Chatting on the phone to let me know he was on his way back, I asked Rob if there had been any more bizarre happenings in the waiting room to keep him amused. He went on to explain the surgery had been quite busy and he had had to wait some time, but said he was kept amused by an air-vented black bag lying at a lady's feet opposite, issuing the sound of an aggravated and very disgruntled cat, which was so irate, the bag appeared to have a life of its own as it bulged and distorted.

Teddy couldn't fathom what this strange black creature could be and sidled a short distance towards it for a quick sniff. Not risking actual contact, he stopped short, quietly growling as the moggy was throwing itself about inside. As it didn't appear to pose any present danger, he left the pulsating bag and returned to sit at Rob's side, keeping watch, just in case. Rob was trying hard not to laugh and Maisie determined she was going nowhere near it. The lady offered no words of comfort to calm her apoplectic moggy and he could only imagine what the vet might face when the angry feline was finally let loose.

Dog Troubles – Teddy's Story

Rob nearly got stuck in a tight space and I had a complete meltdown one morning when we were out with the dogs enjoying a sunny walk alongside the river Verdon. The pathway slices between the river and the Parc de Loisir, a large area, open in summertime to keep the liveliest of kids entertained by providing a massive swimming/boating lake with a diving platform and helter-skelter water slide. Once the kids are fed up with getting wet, they have an enormous choice of activities they can pick, keeping them out of their parents' hair and fully occupied for days. While the little terrors run around in organised chaos, the parents can lounge on the groomed grassy areas under the trees or enjoy a meal in the onsite restaurant. Those adults still in touch with their inner child don't miss out either as they are free to participate if they fancy it.

On that particular morning, we arrived at the large car park and found it lacking cars and occupied by a couple of large bulldozers, excavation equipment and building materials. With the dogs on their leads, we went to find out what was going on. It appeared, now summer had flown, a suitable time to repair or renovate the manmade lake. Where enticing blue water once existed was now a very large hole, on two levels, with a loose gravel base. We were really curious to find out what was going on as we'd never seen the lake drained before.

The lack of any human presence meant there was no one to ask. Disappointed we were unable to assuage our curiosity, we continued along the path towards its furthest point a couple of kilometres away. Both unleashed dogs were enjoying their freedom, sniffing for evidence of other dogs or simply exploring the terrain. Due to the proximity of the stables and the pathway being used for horse riding, we needed to keep a close eye on our hounds. They delight in seeking out and rolling enthusiastically in any noxious animal deposits, fox being a particular favourite. Thankfully, horse didn't prove that appealing and we avoided suffering the results of any such activity, while they avoided a cold shower from the hosepipe.

Moving away from the temptations of poo bathing, Teddy's movements are particularly monitored. He's always mad keen to get into the river, but in October, the water is freezing and moves at a pace around large rocks as it rushes southwards. Eventually, he gets the message and our stress levels return to normal.

On this occasion, the dogs were behaving beautifully as we slowly ambled back towards the car park on our return journey. Just before our destination, Teddy's nose caught the scent of something. He swerved from the path, frantically searching between the huge boulders at the top of the river bank, squeezing his snout into gaps and scrabbling from one side to the other. Rob was up ahead with Maisie as I was trying my utmost to gain the attention of our fixated dog. All at once, he stopped dead, cocked his head to one side, dropped his nose down again and disappeared.

I rushed to the scene to see the entrance of a large concrete drainage pipe and knew instantly where Teddy had gone. On my knees in front of the thing, all I could see was darkness, my panicked voice echoing along it as I called his name. I then heard a whine and knew immediately that Teddy was in trouble. I ran back to the path, screaming Rob's name, telling him he had to come back because Teddy's predicament was serious. Once back, Rob crouched before the entrance and called Teddy. Another whine and the sound of scrabbling paws could be heard, but still no sign of him. We were both in a complete panic. Questions about what we should do if Teddy was trapped inside somewhere were passed back and forth. Would the builders dig the pathway up to try and free him? Should we call for the *pompiers* (the fire and rescue service)? Our heads were in a spin, but for now, it was down to us to do all we could.

I ran across the pathway to investigate where the other end of the pipe might be, but the Parc is fenced and we were limited in our search. I was a snivelling wreck by then, imagining all sorts of horrors awaiting our precious dog. The only choice was for Rob to go in. He manoeuvred himself into the opening, forced to slide on his stomach as space was tight, using the torch on his mobile phone to show the way. With his feet still outside the pipe in case I needed to drag him out, he said he couldn't see Teddy at all but could hear him close by. Then Rob had an idea and instead of shining the light further into the tunnel, turned the light onto his own face. Several seconds later Rob shouted he'd got hold of Ted and slowly dragged him out.

The relief was overwhelming. We cuddled our boy who was shaking with fright. He was slightly wet even though the pipe was dry and seemed as happy to see us as we did him. Maisie had stayed right next to us throughout, seemingly sensing something was amiss, but happy to see Teddy emerge from the darkness. Once Ted was placed on his lead, his whole demeanour was reminiscent of Eeyore, Winnie-the-Pooh's sad donkey friend. He looked very sorry for himself for a while, but a treat lifted his spirits and we knew he'd learned his lesson.

Back in the car, we pondered a few scenarios about Teddy's experience inside the pipe, but it was all guesswork and we'll never know the true facts. We also presumed it might have been the discharge pipe from the manmade lake and were horrified at the thought of him being there when the lake had started to empty. What we do know, is that our old boy Teddy, who has almost lost his sight in one eye, was probably frightened and confused. Shining a light towards him would have dazzled him and worried him further, but once Rob turned the light onto his own face, Teddy recognised his target and headed towards safety.

Next time we go that way, Teddy will be on his lead until well past the danger, though I don't think he'll be tempted to try that little stunt again!

Farewell to the Pizza Hut

As we neared our leaving day, we finally managed a chat with JC, the builder son of Simone and Albert, who was busy working outside their house. A pile of detritus scattered about on the ground below the steps contained the remains of building materials, old kitchen cupboards and an assortment of discarded household items. Much of it had been part of the adjacent pizza hut, the place where we'd spent so many happy times in the presence of our wonderful neighbours. This little building, the holder of so many great memories, had gone and the only things still in situ were the wood burning pizza oven, the BBQ and the low supporting wall. Although we felt a tinge of sadness at its demise, since Albert had passed away it had become neglected and left unused, slowly deteriorating into a ramshackle eyesore. He had constructed it more than three decades previously as a resource for the whole *copropriété,* but once the master of this little venue had slipped away, no one liked to intrude on what was once his domain.

Above this, on level ground, a neat concrete terrace had been laid. The concrete steps leading up to it had received a facelift to match. The old wooden steps, supports and fencing leading up to the front door had been completely replaced with new wood and varnished in a rich oak colour. The front door itself had been relocated further along, the space now occupied by a window. Pretty stone cladding and decorative tiles now adorned the lower wall of the house beside the *sous-sol* door. We had to admit the exterior of the property looked superb and admired the work and effort JC had put into renovating it.

He told us he'd almost completed the work on the interior and had extended the kitchen to the place where the front door used to be. Underneath the new window lay the kitchen sink, allowing the light to flood in and present the magnificent valley view as the backdrop. We've yet to see inside for ourselves, but are sure the whole ground floor was opened up to allow for more space.

Before saying our *au revoirs* we asked after Simone, still living independently in St Tropez where she'd lived her whole married life with Albert, raising their son and daughter. He told us she was in good spirits, but indicated she was getting frail both mentally and physically. We asked him to give her our love.

We waved goodbye to Les Hirondelles, feeling happy that Albert and Simone's little house had been given a new lease of life becoming a home away from home for their extended family. We also knew we would still be welcome to use the pizza oven if we wished, but our pizzas would never match the quality of those prepared by Simone and cooked by Albert.

38

More Teddy Antics

O nce we hit Calais, a short detour *to Blériot-Plage* is usually on our itinerary. This 18 km (11 mile) long beach is made up of fine sand, backed by dunes with a couple of graffiti-covered WW2 bunkers lying slightly askew and partly buried. Lines of groynes are situated at regular intervals, installed to protect the beach from erosion, presenting a hobby photographer like me with plentiful opportunities to practise, especially at sunset when the sun's rays peek through the small gaps between the darkened hard-wood posts, reflecting on the wet sand as the waves steadily wash in and out.

The beach was named after Louis Blériot, the world renowned aviator, who made the first aeroplane flight across the English Channel from this very spot in 1909. Sadly, in present times, it's often the launching point for many rubber boats illegally transporting the desperate in their attempt to reach the UK.

During six months from the beginning of October to the end of March/April dogs are allowed to run freely on what is always their favourite surface, charging around in circles and barking with the sheer joy of it. During this time, Teddy managed to disgrace himself by trotting to the top of a sand dune to enthusiastically roll in something. We knew this as Maisie was focused on his antics. We could just about spy our upside down dog, legs in the air, enjoying this satisfying activity without a care in the world. Rob, who'd been enjoying his relaxing stroll along the beach, suddenly found himself engaging in more strenuous exercise than anticipated, forced to struggle up the dune as fast as possible, fighting the sand shifting beneath his feet, yelling at Teddy to "Stop!" Maisie and I watched from a distance, enjoying the spectacle no end!

He finally reached the top, no doubt feeling a sense of dread at the possible result of Teddy's antics, but it wasn't as expected.

"Grab hold of him!" I yelled towards my aggravated husband.

"What do you think I'm doing!" he yelled back

"What's he rolled in now?"

"It looks like a dead bird!"

The thought of loading Teddy into the car, yet alone the horror of arriving at the hotel reception accompanied by a dog dripping with rotting bird innards, didn't exactly fill me with joy, but once Rob was back at my side with a remarkably clean looking dog, devoid of any grot, I relaxed somewhat. A quick sniff towards him also proved there were no nasty smells ready to assault the unsuspecting either.

"How come he's so clean?"

"The bird was long dead. Anything gunky was long gone. Just a few feathers and a skeleton."

"Thank heavens for that!"

Just as a precaution, Teddy earned himself a good dunking in cold sea water which he was very happy about, but the actual result of his exploits showed up a week later; a bad attack of the mange for him and a serious vet's bill for us!

PART VII

WINTERTIME YARNS

39

More Pet Passport Misery

Before leaving for France on our annual skiing trip, we needed to take the dogs for their standard annual vaccinations against all the nasty diseases that lie in wait in the UK to cause serious illness or death. Both dogs were fine as injections were administered, and the young female vet gave each a quick going over with the stethoscope. She took rather longer when listening to Teddy's heart and I hoped she'd found nothing serious. She revealed he had a heart murmur and wondered why it hadn't been spotted before. We wondered why too. Maybe it's because Teddy hates the vets and after being dragged over the threshold, spends most of his time trying to get out again. We were recommended that Teddy's heart be scanned under sedation to identify exactly how bad it was and to design a suitable treatment plan. From her comments, it seemed Teddy was in danger of dropping dead at any minute and it really gave us a scare. She then asked about symptoms, none of which he'd ever suffered, remaining the slightly mad-cap animal we'd adopted six years previously. I think we must have sounded rather indignant, as she backtracked and eventually asked us to simply monitor him and bring him back if any of the symptoms she'd mentioned became obvious.

Our doggie problems didn't end there as we were subjected to the usual scrutiny when showing their passports at the Tunnel's Pet

Reception, only this time we faced a supervisor who was one of the most obnoxious individuals we'd ever come across. She certainly overdid the 'job's worth', warning us that the passports had not been completed correctly and proceeded to point to a series of empty boxes on one of the pages, demanding they be filled by our French vet while implying she thought he might be a fraud! We were horrified by this and the young girl who was originally dealing with us began to look very uncomfortable on our behalf.

The Ms Trunchbull of Pet Reception then nastily added that she was putting a 'note' on the computer system and if those boxes were **not** completed upon our return, the dogs would **not** be permitted to enter the UK. We told her politely we'd used them for five return journeys, our vet had carried out the corrections previously requested and we had never been refused entry. This went down like a lead balloon and she was having none of it, finally scurrying back to her lair with the expression of a bulldog swallowing a wasp. Her ears must have been burning for the next ten minutes as we headed for the car discussing what a miserable, bad-tempered old bovine she was. Her attitude had been appalling and I'm sure our vet would be delighted to know he was considered a fake. Oh, how we wished we could introduce them.

After this pasting, we were happy to be arriving at our overnight hotel. We'd chosen to give St Omer a miss on this trip and head for a hotel we've used probably more than most and named for the huge pine trees in its grounds. It had changed ownership just before Covid. The previous owners had grown to know us well, but the lady threw in the towel and retired, leaving her son and husband to continue working for the new owner in their previous roles—her husband as chef and her son working front of house in the restaurant. The hotel is in a quiet setting, not too far from the *autoroute* and is unusual as it houses guests in two-storey detached blocks, resembling small houses positioned around the car park, much like a motel, but slightly more upmarket. Some additional accommodation is found in the main hotel building along with the restaurant. This sits in a large, bright room, with huge windows along the wall from which you have a great view of the countryside. A wonderful dinner, a good night's sleep and breakfast set us up for our continued journey towards our second night, which was to be spent in the company of our friends.

Reminiscences With Good Friends

It was great seeing Bob and Sylviane again. Being invited to stay has always been a real treat, especially as Sylviane is a great cook. Bob isn't bad either! The conversation flowed freely over dinner that night. Political and economic matters from both sides of the channel received an airing, confirming that societal doom and gloom was not exclusively the domain of the UK, with France suffering the same cost of living struggles. Our despondency was short-lived lived though, quickly thrown aside in favour of recalling school days shared and tales of youthful antics and neighbourhood capers while growing up on our council estate.

We've talked about these tales many times, but something new always crops up. On this occasion, it concerned our school teachers and their means of punishment. The cane was the weapon of choice for the headmaster, inflicting pain on boys who committed serious offences, such as being consistently badly behaved in class or fighting in the playground. Girls would avoid such brutality in favour of spending weeks in detention and the summoning of parents. We had teachers who were genius potshots with a board rubber or piece of chalk. One in particular used to launch the missile with his back to the pupils, catching the giggling guilty party completely by surprise. Another used to sneak around with a table tennis bat, to be used on the unsuspecting and distracted. A swift, sharp smack on the head with the rubberised side soon returned attention to the work in hand.

It didn't matter what form of physical punishment was meted out back then, we all accepted it as the norm and were never that bothered. The absolute worst was facing the wrath of your parents, who learning of any misdemeanour at school, would deliver the most terrifying diatribe, then enforce house arrest, with no release to go out with your mates for a week and/or a ban on pocket money. It's amazing any of us survived without serious mental problems, but hey, we were tough back then.

Bob has lived for over forty years of his life in France since marrying Sylviane, whom he met while she was in the UK on a school exchange. They are both fluent in each other's languages, but Bob, during our conversations in English, will still unconsciously dig up the buried remains of his Brummie accent that the three of us share. He sounds just like he did at school, but with the odd French verbal intrusion to add confusion. I just envy his ability to jump rapidly from one language to another without drawing breath. Sylviane is much the same.

After breakfast the next morning, we said our goodbyes armed with two hand-made savoury tarts and home-cured sausage. We left with their announcement they might be coming to the UK to visit Bob's brother and hoped this would be realised soon so we'd get the chance to spoil them for once.

40

Off to the Snow

W e'd left fairly early that morning, it being Saturday with half-term holidays in full swing in France and the UK. We were joining the *autoroute* from Lyon to Geneva where there's no escaping the enormous *bouchons* (traffic jams), as everyone appears to be heading for the mountains. It seems an impossibility all these people can be accommodated in the Alpes without their destinations feeling like the crush of fans trying to leave Wembley Stadium on FA Cup Final day. It's a blessing France staggers the February two-week school holiday between three areas, avoiding complete teeth-grinding chaos on the roads and the slopes.

We moved at a snail's pace, the next minute finding the traffic speeding up and able to boot the accelerator before realising we'd been hoodwinked as it all became a crawl once more. We were kept amused by observing a few French drivers who insisted on demonstrating their lack of patience by queue dodging, moving from lane to lane, desperate to gain distance and out-manoeuvre their equally impatient compatriots. We stayed put, grinning when our queue slowly moved forward, passing the plonkers who now found themselves no further forward than when they'd started. After a couple of hours of entertainment and misery, the exit for Grenoble was upon us. We turned off into what was much lighter traffic, finally making decent progress for the remainder of our journey.

We arrived safely, to find the house not quite the freezer we expected due to the lovely weather, but still cold enough to warrant a log fire once we'd unloaded the car. Tasha, Dan and the grandchildren arrived shortly afterwards, having faced the usual flight delays from Heathrow, happy to snuggle down in front of the fire and chat before bed. The girls were soon asleep, exhausted by an early start, saving what was left of their excitement until the following morning when they'd commence ski school.

It wasn't the very early start expected. Lengthy journeys, whether by air or road, can be exhausting, resulting in a lazy lie-in the following morning and a rather slow start to the day. Once any trace of lethargy had fled and breakfast consumed, everyone was raring to go. Our daughter is a planner and takes after me in that regard. The pair of us need to have things researched, scheduled and booked beforehand, so, with her family ski passes and the children's ski school all bought and paid for in advance, the only need was a visit to one of the ubiquitous ski rental shops in the resort further up the valley. They headed off, leaving Rob and me to tidy up and rather languidly make preparations for our own departure, ensuring the dogs had everything they needed before they were left in charge of the house.

Since finding Les Hirondelles and knowing the slopes are just a stone's throw further up the valley, we no longer kill ourselves skiing from dawn to dusk every day as we once did. Back then you needed to make sure you made full use of your expensive weekly ski pass, hotel and flights, grabbing every available minute on the slopes, with just one week to get rid of your skiing obsession before flying home and having to wait until the following year before you could do it all over again. We were also a lot younger then! Nowadays, we stick to half days which include a break to thaw out and stock up on some energy by supping a hot drink and gorging on a sugary waffle.

The first few days of skiing were ridiculously warm for the mountains in winter. The temperatures at the base would rise to 13 degrees centigrade (55 degrees fahrenheit) during late afternoon, leaving the snow lower down turning into what we call 'mashed potato'; a danger to knees whether young or old! Higher up things were much improved where old folks like us could avoid any joint twisting injuries. The whole ski terrain had received tons of snow over the previous couple of weeks, so with extensive snowmaking on the lower slopes and night time temperatures well below freezing, we were reassured that fun in the snow was never going to be off the menu.

There is nothing quite like sunny days on the slopes, whether skiing, boarding, walking or simply sitting outside enjoying lunch surrounded by the most perfect blue and white. Wrapping up in appropriate clothing is a must, except on these rare unusually warm days. We often met our daughter and her family in a car park that leads directly onto the snow at the top of the nursery slope. Standing by the car in blazing sunshine wrapped head to foot in ski gear, struggling to get ski boots on, we'd soon be red faced and sweaty from the effort. Feeling more like the tropics, it was tempting to leave the ski wear behind and head off in our underwear, but knowledge is a precious gift and going higher meant those temperatures were going to feel like the inside of your freezer.

With the grandchildren occupied during the afternoons, their parents could go off and explore the full extent of the resort leaving Rob and me to our own devices, discovering a brand new slope that headed from the top of the Col d'Allos, which became a firm favourite. I also managed a rather spectacular wipe out which thankfully failed to cause any pain or injury. I could only imagine what I looked like as I slid down the steep slope on my back, giggling non-stop at the thought of it. Devoid of skis and poles as they'd flown off in the fall, I finally came to a stop. My attention was then grabbed by the sound of whoops and cheers emanating from the ski lift overhead. Glancing upwards to see the source of the noise, I acknowledged the applause from the group of amused young teens with a wave of my hand. I would have bowed but I'd yet to stand on my feet.

During the week, we never missed our *après ski,* but abandoned our usual haunt after they introduced a cut-off time for those just wanting a drink in favour of those requiring dinner. We discovered another venue back down the valley and were served by a French lad who had spent a year in Birmingham, managing to acquire excellent English without adopting the Brummie accent. We wearily staggered from the bar deciding we didn't fancy spending time over a hot cooker when we got back, so headed across to the permanent pizza van whose menu is extensive and their pizzas mouth-watering. Even vegan Dan was happy.

We spent our last night *en famille* with our regular attendance at the mountainside shindig routinely held at the end of each half-term break. It included exactly the same format as previous years, but the atmosphere is just so infectious, surrounded by happy smiling faces and excited children. It's a great way to round off the week.

The following morning, our little family left for the airport with the house becoming quiet once more. That night, the weather changed and we found ourselves getting excited as fat snowflakes floated past the window and settled on the balcony. Temperatures had dropped to below freezing during the day and were positively arctic at night. Tasha and Dan were really cheesed off having missed bucket loads of fresh snow to ski on, but we had another week to bravely venture out and enjoy it. I say bravely, as the sky was grey and gloomy, leaving us prey to the bitter wind and frequent snow showers that would attack us while stuck on a ski lift, unable to escape or move our limbs to keep warm. At least, with half-term over, the slopes were deserted.

Rob's Day Out

Having finally satisfied our yearning for skiing this year, we packed away all our gear to await next year's adventures, presuming our energy levels and joints allowed it. Our priority now was to get our vet to carry out the additions to the dog passports, as demanded by the she-devil at Pet Reception. We took a forty-minute drive down to find the surgery closed and a notice fixed to the door saying the vet was unwell and not in attendance. It also offered an emergency number for another surgery in Digne les Bains, but we declined the offer. Instead, we took the risky decision to return in a couple of days, hoping he'd be back in residence and recovered from whatever it was he was suffering with. There was one thing wrong with this idiotic decision; our return would be the day before we left for the UK.

Fingers were crossed and nerves stretched as I packed Rob off to do the vet thing. I remained at the house due to my *femme de ménage*, (cleaning lady) role, needing to get things spic and span before we locked up the house. I find I'm better off if Rob is out of the way so I don't have to teach him how to switch on the vacuum.

The phone rang, disrupting my concentration as I was cleaning out the log fire and trying to stop the ash floating everywhere. I answered to hear Rob sounding miffed, telling me the surgery was still closed. I suggested he try the number on the notice pinned to the door. Five minutes later, the phone rang again. I scrabbled off my knees to answer it, having just started battling the filthy grate again.

"What's happened?" I enquired.

"They answered, but can't get the dogs in until next week!" said a frustrated Rob. "Now what!"

"You'll have to drive to Castellane," I said.

"Are you sure there's a vet's? I don't ever remember seeing one."

"I think it's on the outskirts of the town along the road where you found the dentist's surgery. You remember. That time when our local dentist tried to stick your front tooth back in and then you went back 'cause it hadn't worked and caught him having a bit of a leg-over with his nurse."

"Oh yeah. I'd forgotten that. Nearly caught him red-handed. He was a bit flustered and wasn't pleased. Said he was leaving for the day and sent me to the dentist in Castellane instead. Anyway, I'll drive down and see what's what."

"OK, but just ask someone if you can't locate it. Give me a ring when you've found them," I said

One hour later, the phone rings.

"Found it, but it's not where you said it was and they can't fit me in until 3.15 pm. It's only 11.30 am and it isn't worth driving all the way back just to do the whole thing in reverse," said Rob.

"To kill time, why don't you take the dogs for a nice walk? Go and see those manatees I saw with my friends a few years back," I suggested.

"Manatees? What manatees? I remember they had them in Florida, but here? Doubt they're splashing around in the lake." He said with a laugh.

"No, you twit. They're very dead, fossilized millions of years ago. They're actually called *Sirenians*. Sounds like something from *Star Wars* to me. I told you at the time there's a wall of their preserved skeletons, protected with perspex screening. There's a big information board at the site if you're interested. It's a bit of a trek through woodland above Castellane but it's signposted. It's worth seeing and the dogs will love the walk. Then you can grab a sarnie and beer from one of the bars and head for the appointment."

"OK. Worth a try. I'll ring you when I'm out of the vets," said Rob.

Knowing I was in for a long wait, I pressed on with my Mrs Mop impression and finally collapsed a few hours later, grubby, sweaty and tired, but at least all surfaces were clean enough to eat your dinner off. A shower restored my energy and reminded me I needed to stave off hunger with a light lunch followed by doing nothing except lazing on the balcony in the sunshine, wrapped in my warm fleece, with my Kindle for company.

I have no idea how long it was, but I do know the sun was beginning its slide downwards and the temperature drop made me scurry indoors to continue reading. I was eventually summoned by my mobile. A happy Rob informed me he was finally on his way back. The lady vet had really impressed Rob with her efficiency. She informed him she was unable to change or add anything to another vet's comments, but offered to give the dogs a rabies jab each and complete the passport as demanded by the harpy at the tunnel. These were not due for another nine months, but it was deemed safe to top up the dogs for another three years. She also carried out the normal requirements for return to the UK and gave them both the once over. They were judged to be very healthy, Maisie particularly so. Teddy's heart received a check after Rob requested it to confirm the previous diagnosis and rather scary prognosis. She detected a very light murmur, explaining to Rob that it was so tiny as to be completely insignificant and unlikely to affect him to any great degree for the remainder of his life.

"Did you manage to grab a quick snack?" I enquired. "I'll get dinner ready for when you arrive. You must be starving. I know I am, as I only had a piece of quiche for lunch, I'm looking forward to a proper meal."

"Errr. Actually I'm not that hungry."

"Why?"

"Well, it was a bit of a walk with the dogs, and muddy, so I didn't get to see those fossils. Instead, I headed back into Castellane and found this nice restaurant. The owner persuaded me to try the *menu du jour*. Three courses and fabulous! Had a beer to go with it too."

You can imagine this revelation didn't go down too well after my spartan lunch, but at least he had the good grace to sound sheepish!

Two Chats and Sad News

The gap between our two visits to the vet's consisted of the usual shopping for food and dog walking. During our skiing week, we always popped into a supermarket we had to pass on our way to and from the resort. It was just so convenient, but more importantly, the place had completely ripped up the French rule book when it came to shop opening and closing times. In fact, this wonderful *supermarché* would open at 7.00 am every day of the week, refusing to close its doors until 7.00 pm. It was obviously a welcome resource as it was always busy.

This meant we'd had little opportunity to catch Phillipe behind the counter if he was back from his well-earned break, and sadly, we left after not seeing him at all. We knew Olivier wasn't about either as he would be over in Pra Loup, so were surprised when we caught sight of him as we were driving through the town.

We pulled up beside him and had a conversation through the open window of the car. Seems he wasn't working as planned because he'd been skiing, had managed to fall, breaking his collar bone and a couple of ribs in the process. To do this much damage, he'd either attempted the obstacles in the boarders' park or was skiing too fast on a difficult run. After some light-hearted banter reminding him he was no longer a teenager with rubber bones, he laughingly agreed and was still smiling when we pulled away, waving our goodbyes and promising we'd pop down to the restaurant when we returned later in the year. We think Olivier is a bit of a speed merchant anyway as he often takes part in an annual event in October which sees cars of various models, vintages and conditions careering hell for leather up the precipitous route to the Col de St Michel! The route makes my stomach churn and knuckles turn white at a snail's pace, so I think they're all slightly insane to attempt it at high speed. One year we had the opportunity to stand at the finish line, high above the valley. I think a souped-up mini won if my memory serves me correctly.

Our leaving day arrived and while throwing luggage into the back of the car, JC happened to drive past and stopped to talk. He could see we were leaving and asked when we'd be back, so I regaled him with the exciting time we were due to have this current year with big birthdays, a big wedding anniversary and a celebratory cruise. Whether he needed to hear all this information seems doubtful, but he listened politely until I'd divulged everything except my dress size! I did finally tell him that all this partying meant we couldn't make it back until the summer. He in turn told me it was his birthday that weekend. He was in his late fifties and as the house was finished and all the rubbish cleared from outside, leaving the area pristine, his wife, children, their partners and grandchildren would be arriving later for a two-day get-together. He explained he hadn't room to accommodate them all, but as he was friends with the couple who owned the adjacent property, they kindly were allowing the overflow of family to lodge there. He was obviously thrilled at the prospect of sitting down to a big family dinner, enjoying the food, the wine and the company. We continued to talk about the joys of sharing time with family and before we said our goodbyes, I remembered to offer him our condolences. Prior to us leaving the UK, Gilbert emailed to say the wonderful Simone had passed away in late January.

We will forever cherish the memories of this gorgeous lady, her sense of mischief, her love for Albert and for the kindness and care she extended towards us, our family and friends. Another lovely soul gone from this world.

Grandad Gets a Surprise

While securing the house and emptying the water from the system, Rob found himself mobbed by a swarm of gnats, midges, or some other breed of flying miniature annoyances. He'd just opened the tiny hatch positioned under the balcony, behind which are the two small taps he needed to access in order to complete the job when, without warning, he suddenly found himself immersed in a cloud of tiny irritants. I didn't witness the event but can imagine the scene. He no doubt attempted to hold his breath to avoid inhaling several into his lungs while trying to fight the little blighters off without knocking himself unconscious on the balcony beams.

It does kind of serve him right. The week before, when our granddaughters were playing outside, they ventured into what they call their secret cave, the *sous-sol*. Not long afterwards they arrived in the house, approaching Grandad Rob, curious to know why we stored all 'that stuff' down there and what was it all anyway. After giving them an explanation that seemed to satisfy their need to know, they then announced the 'cave' was full of lots and lots of mosquitoes too. Rob brushed it off, stating that mosquitoes don't live in the mountains because it's too cold. With that, they skipped off to amuse themselves elsewhere and left Rob to find out the truth a week later. Silly Grandad!

41

Homeward Bound

We headed north towards Burgundy, encountering light traffic now that every school in Europe had returned to educate our future adults, leaving locals, workers and people like us to occupy the *autoroutes* at leisure. The sun travelled along with us and bedded down as we arrived in Bèze, a beautiful village to the northeast of Dijon, registered as one of the *Plus Beau Villages de France*. We've stayed there on countless occasions on our homeward run, usually spending the night in a large *auberge*, but it had recently changed hands and the new incumbents strangely decided not to open the restaurant on Fridays, and you've guessed it, it was Friday. The only other establishments serving food in this tiny place were a little pizzeria and the dining rooms of two smaller lodgings. Thankfully, I'd done my research before leaving the UK and booked one of the alternatives in advance. This was housed in an old building right on the street. Limited parking was available across the road beyond a tiny square area which the hotel uses for outdoor dining in summer, watched over by the *mairie* occupying one side.

We awoke the next morning to find the sun shining and the smell of coffee wafting up the stairs towards our room. We temporarily ignored the temptation, needing to take the dogs for a short walk before grabbing breakfast. Heading outside, the weather was balmy for early March and the blossom was already in full bloom. Bèze is really beautiful with pretty homes built of local stone, some of which hover right next to the water, their walls dipping into the crystal clear River Bèze. The whole place reminds us of our own Cotswold villages.

That morning, I was anxious to head towards the impressive seventh century abbey running the whole length of the main square and sitting perpendicular to the river. Its round tower and conical-shaped roof, typical of Burgundian architecture, stood prettily on the river bank. A lovely modern sculpture placed alongside and cherry trees in bloom on the opposite bank created a tailor-made scene for photography. The abbey was the reason Bèze exists, the village growing steadily around it since medieval times, but obviously, someone called a halt before it morphed into a town. A thirteenth century building, once holding the 'école monastique, still remains, attached to the abbey, but its current use remains a mystery, to us anyway.

Satisfied with my efforts with the camera, we headed back to the hotel, but I had to stop once more as we passed by an ancient manor house. Tall, rusting wrought iron gates guarded the entrance, with a gravel driveway, lined with high hedges, leading to the building itself. It could have been a beautiful home once, but neglect was obvious. The cream-coloured façade had faded, now covered in some kind of climbing plant, lacking of any greenery. The red-tiled roof looked sound enough, but marked by age. The shutters were rotting, the once bright blue now faded to a whisper. Two concrete columns, looking rather incongruous, stood at the front and a main entrance appeared to be non-existent. All we could spy from our distant viewpoint was a small wooden door, the same shade as the shutters, standing open alongside a yawning gap. It was too far away to see what was inside the impenetrable darkness but looked like a large storeroom or even a garage. We surmised it might once have been the grand entrance deserved by this manor house, but no longer. I felt quite sad to see this beautiful property, the river running directly behind it, reduced to a shabby replica of its old self and hoped its magnificence would soon be restored.

"Do you think anyone lives there?" I asked Rob

"Possibly, because the gravel driveway looks well used."

"It's such a shame. Perhaps the owners can no longer afford its upkeep."

"Or maybe it's fallen foul of French inheritance laws and left to distant family members who are arguing about what to do with it." Rob pondered.

"Doesn't explain who's living there now though does it."

"Well, unless you can get through those gates and knock on the door, you're not going to find out. C'mon, let's go grab some breakfast. It finishes at 9.30 am so we'd better get a move on."

We arrived at the hotel's dining room in good time and found the buffet breakfast had been raided to almost total extinction, leaving us to make do with what was left. As Madam made no offer to refurbish the miserable offerings, we drank a lot of coffee and cleared the remains.

Before leaving the village, we strolled towards the source of the river Bèze along the footpath, bounded on one side by plane trees whose proportions confirmed their great age. The water was beautifully clear, with patches of aquatic grasses swaying just below the surface, providing the ducks with plenty of upside-down foraging as they happily paddled and quacked their way upstream. The river's visible life begins at the foot of a semi-circular wall, framing the 10 metre (33 feet) width of the waters. A tall cliff provides the backdrop. In the middle of the shallow river bed is a fissure where the clear water emerges from the deep, causing small swirls on the surface before it begins its 31 kilometre (19.4 miles) journey onwards towards the river Soane.

The source is fed from an underground lake in the Crétanne Cave, 45 metres underground (148 feet). Visitors can descend to the chamber and be taken by boat, pulled along by a series of ropes, across the lake to admire the stalagmites and stalactites. We've yet to venture into the *Grottes du Bèze* as we're always time-limited, the attraction not opening until 11.00 am but determined it's another necessity to be added to our list of must-sees.

One thing we did find was a rather scary image, placed on a nearby notice board, showing the source from 20th December 1913 when a major outburst thrust huge amounts of water through the fissure, creating a boiling cauldron of swirling, frothing waves. We've yet to find out how or why this occurred and what was done to stem the waters to prevent it from happening again.

A stroll back along the pathway, waving goodbye to our enthusiastic ducks, we headed towards a new footbridge, leading us over the river to wander through the lovely gardens on the opposite bank before returning to the car and making our way towards our final night in France.

Police and Pet Reception

Our last stop was our usual hotel, where the French police seem to spend much of their time. The sun had smiled upon us for most of our journey which had happily proved leisurely and stress free. As we often do, we paused for a while at a hypermarket just outside Reims to refuel and stock up on some French delicacies, including Rob's very smelly cheese and several bottles of wine.

Heading towards our overnight premises with darkness descending, the temperature plunging and rain threatening, we shelved any idea of beach walking and doggie derring-do in favour of a warm hotel room and dinner.

Booking in at reception, I spied a member of the French police force, leaving me to wonder if a raid was imminent or if some fugitive was lying low in the hotel. He was joined by another, but they were far too relaxed to be leaping into action any time soon. Later, installed in the dining room eating our evening meal, we were surprised to see them again, joined by four of their compatriots settling in at the table next to ours, dressed in casual gear having left the guns and stab vests in their rooms. Most were built like *The Terminator*, sporting biceps bigger than the width of my thighs, but amusingly, these beefy guys were wearing identical flip-flops. Had they been bought as a job lot we wondered, or had the French police adopted them as regulation footwear for when not on duty? There was absolutely no way we were going to ask!

It was crunch time. We were standing at the Pet Reception awaiting judgment. Ms Nasty was nowhere in sight. Instead, we were greeted by a pleasant young lady who took the proffered Pet Passports, examined them closely and handed them back with a smile, saying we really shouldn't be using them, as it is necessary to wait four weeks after the rabies jab before they become valid, but said not to worry, all was fine and bid us a pleasant journey. We hadn't a clue about the four-week thing but were incredibly grateful to this young woman who reminded us that a poor attitude and rudeness was thankfully the realm of a few.

PART VIII

BONUS CHAPTER -
ONCE UPON A TIME

42

One Last Travel Story

As committed Francophiles, we have spent years exploring the various regions within this beautiful country and can boast about spending time in most, sometimes a flying visit and at other times deciding on a lengthier stay. We're frequently asked by the curious and those unfamiliar with the country to recommend a suitable holiday destination. Inevitably, we get asked, "Well, what's your favourite place?" For the unaware, the answer needs to be approached with extreme caution to avoid influencing their decision. The last thing we want is for the disgruntled and disappointed to return and blame us for persuading them to head for the mountains instead of the beach.

For us, our explorations have always been joyous and we've loved just about everywhere we've been, carefully researching what we needed to see or experience beforehand. One particularly stands out, only because we were unaware of its existence until I read a book; a book that described the events which took place there during WW2 and became the initial reason we both wanted to visit.

I've always had a fascination with WW2, probably because my parents lived through it. Mum worked nights for the duration of the war in a Birmingham factory, its main purpose shifted in favour of contributing to the war effort by producing parts for the Spitfire. With men off fighting, women were recruited to keep things going. Dad was a driver in the army, eventually put in charge of a military ambulance. He and his ambulance were sent to help liberate the notorious concentration camp of Bergen Belsen. My dad, like many, never spoke about his experiences, preferring to keep the horrors of war to himself. What I did learn came from snippets he'd told my mother, but the desire to learn more has always remained with me.

Years before buying Les Hirondelles, we would head south from Grenoble, using the Route Napoleon and for all those years we never knew what lay beyond the wall of impregnable mountains that loomed alongside us across the valley. This turned out to be the Vercors Massif, situated between the valleys of the rivers Drôme and Isère in the Rhône Alpes region. The Massif itself is like a plateau with its valleys and towns nestled a few hundred metres below the encircling mountains, themselves soaring between 800 metres (2,600 feet) and 1,200 metres (3,900 feet) above the surrounding areas. I'm so glad I read that book as it convinced us to add on some extra days and divert there on our homeward trip two years before Covid's arrival shocked the world. Here's the story.

The Vercors

The sun was blazing down as we pulled away from our little home, its shutters now closed tight until our return. We headed north along our usual route, eventually turning off towards the commune of Die (pronounced Dee), the gateway to the Parc Naturel Régional du Vercors. Die is an ancient settlement and amongst its inhabitants were the well-travelled Romans whose occupation is still visible today thanks to the ramparts and the St Marcel Gate built a long, long time ago in the third and fourth centuries. I can still hear those famous words from the hilarious *Life of Brian* as spoken by Reg. "What have the Romans ever done for us?" Well, they were certainly a busy lot and seemed to have popped up all over the place, leaving evidence of their building work for future generations to stumble across and admire. Anyway, let's get back to Die, apart from a rich cultural heritage, it is famous for the production of Clairette de Die AOC. *Appellation d'Origine Contrôlée,* is government certification ensuring that all wines and other food stuffs are produced in the region of origin using traditional methods. Clairette is a fruity and quite sweet version of a sparkling wine. We didn't get the chance to explore or buy any on this visit, though we have had a drink of the frizzy stuff in the past. It's a bit too sweet for our tastes, but not bad for the occasional drink on a summer's day. With no time to linger, we pressed on. It was now late afternoon and we'd already enjoyed a short pause earlier to allow freedom from the confines of the car and a chance for a short stroll in the sunshine with the dogs.

Leaving Die behind, the road started to seriously climb towards the top of the Glandasse mountain, meandering between densely forested slopes completely devoid of any human habitation, to eventually arrive at a viewpoint where we gazed back in the direction we'd travelled, able to see the tiny outline of the 23 kilometre (14 mile) road that had brought us to this spot high above. A short drive, after taking photos of the view, led us over the Col de Rousset and then downhill to follow the valley road. The weather remained sunny and the temperatures were soaring, the heat settled within the surrounding mountains like water in a pool. We experienced just how hot it was when, just below the Col, we negotiated around hordes of parked cars lining the road and stopped a short distance away to find out what was proving such an attraction. We discovered the vehicle occupants enjoying some cooling watery fun in what appeared to be a wide expanse of shallow river. I'm sure Teddy would have been delighted to join them, but he was denied this pleasure and dragged reluctantly back to the car to enable us to continue our journey revelling in the delights of air con.

We arrived in the early evening at the *Hotel et Restaurant de Musee du l'Eau* in the tiny and spectacular village of Pont-en-Royans. I'd checked this quirky place out before booking, wondering about the museum of water included in the name. Whatever it was, at least we were allowed free entry and made a promise to ourselves to visit before we left. Another quirk of this quite basic little hotel was its position, perched right on the cliff edge with the Bourne River running below. The huge terrace adopted the same precarious stance, thankfully with secure fencing along its edge so excited mutts like ours wouldn't wind up receiving a surprising and speedy plunge into the river.

We'd booked half board, making our stay a bit cheaper, knowing we wouldn't be tempted to buy the most expensive stuff on the menu. That first night turned out to be a real hoot! It was party time on the terrace, the tables laid ready for dinner, a band playing medleys of songs to guests with plenty of room for dancing if you fancied it. We were also given a menu and instructed to pick whatever we wanted from it (it was a small menu) and wine was free of charge for a single carafe. We ordered rosé and nearly died when a whole litre was delivered by our cheerful waiter. Our travel weariness skedaddled rather sharpish allowing us to enjoy a very long and happy evening culminating in a dog walk down to the river after dark, looking back at the bright lights shining from the cliff top, reflecting in the waters of the river and thinking how very lucky we were to have discovered this little place.

WW2 Explorations

Next morning, over breakfast, we mapped out our explorations for the following three days, starting with the Resistance Museum. The story of what happened in this location during WW2 is too involved to explain here, but it's both fascinating and harrowing in equal measure. From memory, here is a very, very brief summary that really doesn't do it justice.

The Allies decided to combine many of the resistance cells into a more effective fighting force, placing them on the Vercors Massif. It was deemed the perfect spot to hold up German troops heading northwards to join forces with those at Calais, having been tricked into believing the allies would choose it for their major invasion. The Massif was considered impregnable, its mountains impossible for German battalions to scale and with only three accessible routes in, would be easy for the *Maquis* (the name given to rural resistance fighters) to block. The allies made regular air drops at night including much needed weaponry and general supplies. The Germans failed all attempts to access the Vercors and the resistance fighters succeeded in causing major disruptions to the German army machine. Then it all went pear-shaped. Weapons urgently requested didn't arrive due to bad weather and messages received were lost or remained sitting on desks in London and Algiers, unread until too late; it was a shameful display of disorganisation. The Germans then developed gliders and flew in soldiers to do their worst. Citizens fled their homes and the two military hospitals transferred injured fighters from both sides into a cave in the mountains for safety. The *Maquis* fought hard but without heavy weapons, they finally succumbed and the temporary hospital was duly discovered. The injured were shot, others were taken and executed elsewhere and the nurses were deported. The town of La Chapelle-en-Vercors was destroyed. Leaders of the *Maquis* who survived the onslaught were eventually captured and dragged off to be interrogated and finally executed.

If interested in reading in detail about the whole debacle, then the book that piqued our interest is *The Cruel Victory* by Paddy Ashdown.

Our visit to the museum proved really interesting, containing many black and white images of the battle itself, the members of the resistance, their leaders and those who worked for them in the surrounding villages beyond the Vercors. It was definitely worth the entrance fee and, as always with these things, very thought-provoking and sad. Once outside, Rob was impressed by the ingenuity of the Germans, examining the aerodynamics of the glider exhibit, but that's because he's an engineer and can't help but appreciate such things. All I saw was a strange wooden flying contraption, whose development was focused on evil intent.

In bright sunshine, we followed the road towards the Memoriél de la Résistance en Vercors, stopping to see the cemetery on the way, where many of those brave souls are buried, some just boys. We were reminded of how lucky we are to have been born post WW2.

Next was the visit to the memorial itself, perched just below the Col de la Chau, the point at which many of the fighters, male and female, had a clandestine camp. It's certainly not your usual type of memorial and proved really unexpected, it being a long, low building that curves around the contours of the hillside forming a loose S shape. It was perfectly melded into its environment with the flat roofs planted with grass and shrubs. As dogs were *interdit*, ours had to stay in the car, parked in the shade, while we went to find out what it was all about. Our first stop was to admire the extensive view across the valley, an information board providing us with facts about what we could see. Then we headed inside for a walk along the concourse to explore, but without the headphones and commentary, we couldn't participate in the immersive experience advertised. It would have helped enormously as so much of what we were looking at and puzzling over would have been explained.

"It's such a shame we can't do it. I had no idea it was so big. It could take hours to absorb all of this."

"I know," said Rob, "but we can always come back again at some point. If we want to squeeze in our planned visit to the Grottes de la Luire we need to get going before it closes and we've a lengthy drive back to the hotel. If we don't leave now, we'll be getting back too late for dinner."

The dogs were pleased to see us return and even happier when we gave them a short walk and a treat before bundling them into the car once again for the journey towards our next stop.

Our final stop, the *Grottes de la Luire* (Cave of Light) proved quite an experience. Prominently displayed at the cave's yawning entrance was a plaque commemorating those who perished at the site during WW2; those brave souls who believed the huge chambers that existed within would be well-hidden. It was hard to imagine seriously injured soldiers and medical staff coping in such an environment and ultimately facing the horrors of discovery after a German aircraft spotted a red-cross flag that revealed the hospital's secret location.

Before commencing our journey underground, our group were presented with a lantern containing a candle, the only source of light throughout much of the tour. The point of this primitive exercise was to replicate the experience of the original explorers. The difference, of course, was that we had an expert guide who led us safely through the dark interior, occasionally shining a torch onto interesting stalactite and stalagmite formations and warning us if we were approaching any slippery, narrow or sloping areas. To be honest, the pathway was fairly solid, after hundreds of tourists had tramped through it and we all made it out unscathed.

The guide's commentary had continued throughout and although we didn't understand all of it, he did manage to speak some English when we needed it. He spoke of prehistoric inhabitants and initial explorations by speleologists, saving the scary bit for when we were perched on a narrow bridge that was crossing a narrow, 30-50 metre deep shaft (94-168 feet). Shining a light down for effect, everyone fell rather silent except for a few nervous giggles, though the kids in the party were loving it. He explained that in heavy rain the whole place floods at mind-numbing speed, the water forcing its way through the shaft to completely flood the chamber in which we were standing, taking just twenty minutes. That got us all talking! The cave system is closed when heavy rain is forecast and thankfully, drowning wasn't on the itinerary that day as the sun was shining.

Those people mad enough to enjoy exploring the unknown in pitch darkness are advised to check the forecast before entering this enormous system of huge chambers and passages. Such is the risk that an alarm has been installed, but the speed at which the flood occurs means it's a race to make it out in time. It gave us the shudders just thinking about it. Explorers seem to be attracted to this death trap obviously seeking recognition for locating the source of the underground river and finding out where all those passages eventually lead. All this is unknown at present. Not our idea of fun.

That night, we enjoyed a perfect dinner under a sky filled with stars, the soft hum of conversation from fellow diners and the gentle murmur of the river passing by below providing the backdrop, the perfect contrast to the noisy revelry of the previous night and the perfect relaxation after our day's explorations and adventures.

Day two was bright, but not the brilliant sunshine of the past couple of days. To be honest, it was a relief to escape the heat for a while. Our peaceful breakfast on the terrace that morning was shockingly interrupted by the awful cries of a dog in pain, coming from below us by a small river crossing along the top of a weir. I peered over the fencing to see a lovely retriever being attacked by another dog of questionable breed. The retriever was doing its best to escape, but the aggressor was determined to do its worst. I was just about to run quite a distance down to help, when a brave guy appeared and managed to save the day by hitting out at the assailant, who, after a bit of a standoff, slunk away to who knows where. The retriever made its exit in the opposite direction, towards the houses that lined the banks of the river downstream. Me and Rob were really concerned about what we'd witnessed and wondered who would allow such an aggressive dog to prowl about unfettered, worrying about the safety of our own dogs. Thankfully, we never saw it again.

After our WW2 visits the previous day, we decided to concentrate on the natural wonders the Vercors is famous for. We'd already been astonished by Pont en Royan's ancient riverside houses with their balconies precariously suspended on timber struts high above the gorge of the Bourne River. Others possessed walls that stretched from on high to below the river's surface, leaving their remaining neighbours to teeter on the edge of the craggy rock face. To stand on the river bank and gaze upwards begs the question why build in such a perilous spot? And how on earth did they achieve these marvels all those years ago? They weren't even Roman!!

Our first port of call was to be the Grottes de Choranche, which necessitated a drive part-way through the Gorges de la Bourne. The route is truly spectacular, passing through a narrow tunnel blasted through the limestone and continuing past the Châtelus, a huge crescent of sheer cliff face, its feet buried in verdant forest and its head fringed with a neat line of trees, as though planted by some master gardener. A silver thread of water, we later found to be the Bournillon waterfall, plunging 300 metres (nearly 1,000 feet) down the face, disappearing into the trees below. It was a sight to behold and we would stop on our return journey to gaze across the void and take the essential photos!

We finally reached our destination, parked and went to find out if dogs were allowed. We guessed it would be ok. The French don't seem to mind, but I doubt we'd get away with it in the UK. By now it had started to drizzle, so it seemed the perfect place to escape a soaking, swapping it for the chance to freeze as the temperature underground required something warmer to wear. Now deeming ourselves as 'Grottes' experts, we'd wisely come prepared.

It was a completely different experience to the primitive, but interesting Grottes de la Luire. Our guide led us around this wonder of nature for over an hour describing the human history and geology as we followed along. In places, the walls were painted by subtle lighting in a rainbow of muted colours designed to emphasise the contours of the ancient limestone, then to reflect in the underground pools and the river that fed them. One cavern housed a ceiling crowded with impossible numbers of delicate 'straw stalactites', the like we'd never seen before. I remember gasping in awe at this incredible shimmering spectacle of crystalline whiteness.

One of the stranger things we came across was an exhibit lurking in a glass case positioned alongside a stunning turquoise lake. This turned out to be an Olm. We'd never heard of such a creature, even having David Attenborough regularly educating us on the world's wildlife. Apparently, at 35 centimetres long, (nearly 14 inches) it's the largest predator in the subterranean world, though what it feeds on in those dark depths I can't remember or imagine. The best way to describe it is to say it resembles a newt, a very weird-looking one with a snaky body and tiny legs. It's also blind, devoid of pigmentation, can go without food for months and is known to live up to eighty years old. Of course, I took a picture as I doubted I'd ever see one again. Maybe I should send it to David, just in case he missed this one.

As we approached the end of the tour, we were shown into the Cathedral Chamber, the name giving a clue to its vastness. In the middle was another beautiful lake and overlooking it was a bank of seating. Our tour members were ushered into place, then the lights were switched off. In total darkness, we sat silently wondering what to expect. Then a beam of light lit a tiny rock pool accompanied by the soft notes of splashing water, the sound projected around the enormous cavern. Next came the cry of a baby and the story of human habitation began, unfolding purely through light and sound. It was entrancing and beautifully done. A wonderful way to end our visit.

Blinking our way back into the brightness, we were happy to find the drizzle had disappeared, so lingered to read the information boards, followed by a stroll along a trail leading us through a rock tunnel towards a gentle veil of water falling quietly into the depths. The sky was slowly brightening as the rain clouds moved away, the air gathering warmth once again as we made our way to the car and headed back.

Water Tasting

It was our last day and the time had come to explore the water museum next to the hotel. It was small and filled with information and descriptions of watery origins, processes and uses. A brief wander around the exhibits led us to the entrance of the tasting room and, extremely curious, we decided to join the next session.

"This is bonkers," said Rob. "Water is just water isn't it?"

"I'm intrigued. Just look at all those bottles lined up. Must be fifty or more, all different brands, shapes and sizes. This is going to be an experience." I replied.

"Yeah, you're not joking. At least you won't be staggering out of there feeling the worse for wear as you've done on the odd wine-tasting occasion."

"That was years ago and it was your fault for filling up my glass each time."

"Ha! Didn't force you to drink it though, did I?" Said Rob, grinning.

It appeared we weren't the only curious folks about as around ten others joined the session, seated at small tables. The water expert proceeded to open a bottle, explain its country of origin and pour a tiny sample into glasses for us to taste. There appeared some disbelieving expressions dotted about the room, ours included, but it seemed most were trying to order their faces into some semblance of serious concentration. Glasses were distributed by two assistants, and we were then instructed to try a little, which surprisingly tasted like water. Another bottle was quickly opened with samples delivered to the tables.

"Try it, then taste the first one again," said the enthusiastic expert.

We did as we were told and were amazed, it tasted subtly different. We went on to sample bottled spring water from the US, the UK, France, Italy, Canada and a host of other places and regions I can't remember. Each had a unique taste, some very markedly so, with attendees discussing the qualities of what they were tasting and choosing favourites. Our expert did a great job explaining why each was so different, in exactly the same way a *viticulteur* might explain the subtleties of his wine. It had been a real eye-opener and we all left feeling a lot more clued up on the merits of water.

"Well that was a surprise," I said,"I never thought water could taste so very different."

"Neither did I. Does this mean we can save money now you'll be choosing water rather than wine with dinner in future?"

"Now you're being silly," I said to Rob, "I wouldn't go that far!"

The End

Au Revoir et à bientôt, peut-être?

February 2023 marked exactly twenty years to the day since we moved into Les Hirondelles, the description of which is fully explored in my first book, *French Dreams, Dogs and a Dodgy Motor*. This year also marks a watershed in our family lives as we hit a special *anniversaire de mariage* and big birthdays too, though we were only kids when the wedding took place, so we aren't quite over the hill just yet!

Looking to the future, as long as our health keeps up with our intentions, we will continue to visit our little French home regularly, exploring our valley and its mountains throughout the seasons. We will also head out to discover new or re-visit familiar destinations throughout France and the rest of the world. Maisie and Teddy will always accompany us on our French trips, though Teddy is now eleven years old and Maisie is nine. Whatever time they both have remaining, we will continue to give them the best life we can.

We hopefully have many years left before Old Father Time catches up with us and we're determined to keep living life to the full.

Watch this space. Maybe, there'll be more to tell ...

A Review

I sincerely hope you enjoyed reading my book and thank you for buying it. I would greatly appreciate it if you could leave a review on Amazon. Your feedback will help my book become more visible and will help other readers decide if this is the book for them. It means so much to Indie authors like me.

Thank you so much!

Amazon link: https://bit.ly/French-Tales

Books by Jane Smyth

Our French Odyssey, Book 1
French Dreams, Dogs and a Dodgy Motor

Our French Odyssey, Book 2
French Tales, Travels and Two Fox Terriers

Contacts and Links

Connect with the author

Email: authorjanesmyth@gmail.com

Images

For the curious, an online album of images to accompany the tales and places mentioned in this book can be found on:

www.authorjanesmyth.co.uk

We Love Memoirs

If you'd like to chat with Jane and other memoir authors and readers, do join the Facebook group We Love Memoirs, often called the friendliest group on Facebook.

www.facebook.com/groups/welovememoirs/

Acknowledgements

Writing a book is often the easy part, but ensuring it is beautifully presented and fit to publish is down to a whole cast of people who deserve my most grateful thanks.

To Sue Bavey who perused the manuscript with a microscopic eye, finding all those silly errors, correcting my grammar and advising on improvements and additions.

To Victoria Twead and her colleagues at Ant Press who have done a wonderful job in making it look the best it could possibly be and doing all the hard work to bring this book to print. Your patience and advice has been invaluable.

To Vikki Davies from VC Book Covers who once again designed exactly what I wanted, following the theme set by the first book in the series.

To the We Love Memoirs site, a community of memoir authors and fans across the world who help spread the word and are always on hand to answer a question or give an opinion.

To Gilbert and Annie, our 'French' neighbours, who have proved to be the most kind and generous of people. They never fail to lend a helpful hand when needed and ensure we get frequent invitations for apéritifs!

To my friends, who are always there when needed and will be first to read this book.

Finally, special thanks to my amazing family: my grown children, Natasha and Ben, generous, kind and loving, joined by Dan and Nikki, their 'other halves' who have become such a huge part of our family. Love you all. Next, the stars that are my granddaughters, Georgia, Marni and Freja, who continue to bring so much joy and laughter into my life, it's impossible to measure. Finally, it's Rob, my long-time husband, best granddad, best dog dad and quite simply, my best friend. What would I do without you.

And finally, I have to mention Maisie and Teddy, our Fox Terriers. I know they can't read, but I'm sure they'll welcome a treat or two instead, just to show they're appreciated and loved, and for providing enough ammunition to be used in this book!

About the Author

Jane was born in Birmingham, and remains a Brummie at heart although she has lived in north Worcestershire for many years. She worked as a lecturer at a college in the West Midlands for most of her career, starting out teaching secretarial subjects and having to re-educate herself every few years as technology and computers gradually took over.

By the end of her career, she held the position of Senior Teacher and lecturer in IT. She also has qualifications in photography and fitness instruction, the latter she no longer uses, saying she much prefers being a participant rather than the teacher.

Happily married, she and her husband Rob have two children, three granddaughters and currently two fox terriers. They share their time between the UK and their little house in the Alpes de Haute Provence.